la famiglia

ITALIAN TALES

RoseMarie Navarra

Ordering Information:
    For details, contact info@lafamigliabook.com.
Print ISBN: 9780692037263
eBook ISBN: 9781087947396
Printed in the United States of America
    by: small packages press
    First Edition
Design, production, editing, and illustration credits:
    Book design and production: small packages, inc
        smallpackages.com
    Cover and interior illustrations: Greg Correll

PRAISE FOR LA FAMIGLIA

"Come, pull up a chair, you are invited to *Mangia*! These Italian tales are set in the Hudson Valley, New York cities of Beacon and Newburgh. The stories are a family's full menu of joys, intrigues, disappointments, and grief. I especially savored the stories of the women, who each in their unique way, sometimes funny, sometimes sad, come to terms with being female in a mid-20th century Italian family. RoseMarie Navarra, thank you for the invitation, I enjoyed the feast and so will you."

— Kate Hymes, *poet*
Founder/Leader, Wallkill Valley Writers' Workshops

"*A tavola non si invecchia.* (You don't get old at the table.) Not at this table anyway. Not with this family, as portrayed in these heartfelt stories of richly remembered characters. With loads of heart, humor and truth, Rosemarie Navarra's delicious tales instantly engage with nostalgia and demonstrate the power of her frank, evocative storytelling. *La Famiglia* will capture readers at the front door of Grandpa's Barbershop and keep them engaged to the pure chaos of Christmas morning at Grandpa's house. Along the way, this collection of vibrant memories offers an inspiring lesson on how families can unite to become a survival place to learn how to become tough enough to survive."

— Christine Crawfis
Managing Director, Mohonk Mountain Stage Company

la famiglia
ITALIAN TALES

for my mother and her sisters

Prologo

EVERYWHERE I LOOKED there were Italians.

Italian men playing Bocce, drinking homemade wine, bossing their wives around. Italian women cooking and cooking, serving and serving, and forever cleaning up. Italian grandmothers waving wooden spoons, chasing children who try to sneak meatballs before dinner.

Italian great-aunts all in black, forty years after their husbands died; Italian uncles in fancy clothes, with more money than they could have legitimately earned—and my aunts, oh my aunts! So emotional, so funny, so beautiful.

On Sunday afternoons we all went to Grandma and Grandpa's, where there would often be an Italian musicale. My grandfather playing the concertina or the violin, my uncles playing guitar, accordion, mandolin, and my grandmother and aunts singing. My grandfather's beautiful tenor voice on "Torno A Surriento," "o Sole Mio," "Santa Lucia," and other songs by request

Everyone would listen and cry. Then everyone would eat and the men would drink wine.

Italian weddings with food for an army—and a terrible band, playing the Tarantella for the women to dance to. Fights breaking out between new in-laws, infants being nursed, babies crying, children throwing candy-coated almonds at each other. Mothers of grooms crying throughout, whispering to whoever would listen to how the bride can't cook, they'll have ugly children, and she'll never make him happy. Then everyone would eat and the men would drink wine.

Christenings, where the uncles put twenty-dollar bills into the hands of infants and old women made the hand gestures to protect the baby from the evil eye. Then everyone would eat and the men would drink wine.

At funerals, widows flung themselves on to coffins and tried to jump into open graves, held back by pallbearer uncles. Then everyone would eat and the men would drink wine.

Aunts fighting and crying on the phone, uncles swearing in Italian—and constant talk of respect: no respect, fake respect, too late for respect, never got respect, never shows respect, doesn't deserve respect, didn't earn respect, died without respect. No respect for hard work, no respect for the dead; can't respect a lazy man, can't respect a woman who can't cook, can't respect a man who can't hold his wine, can't respect a woman who drinks, can't respect a poor housekeeper, can't respect a bad driver...

Then there were all the rationales for why Italians are superior to all others: Poles are stupid; the Irish are drunks; French are dirty; the Jews are cheap; Hungarians are hotheads. Russians are crazy; Germans are evil; the Japanese are cruel and Turks are monsters. English are heartless, the Spanish are liars, and there's no such thing as an American (because every American is originally from somewhere else.)

And pronouncements:

Italians who marry non-Italians are stupido.

Single women who leave their parents' homes
and live on their own are *puttanas* (whores).

A man who gives in to a woman is a *vigliacco* (coward).

A man who gets drunk is an *imbarazzo* (embarrassment).

A man who doesn't work is a *mezzo calzetta*
(worthless person) or a *barbone* (bum).
Never marries? Barbone!
A woman who never marries is a *zitella* (spinster)
or *disastra* (disaster).
No man likes a woman who is too *intelligente*
(smarter than he is).

And the importance of the proper preparation of certain foods:
the sauce, the meatballs, the *braciole*, the lasagna—the list is long,
covering all Italian dishes, as well as critiques of homemade wines:
too sweet, too sour, too dry, too tart, too heavy, too light, aged too
long, too short, improperly made…or just bad grapes—too green,
too ripe, too many stems, bad soil.

Or the worst and fatal flaw: it's turned to VINEGAR! (This
fatal flaw is spit out while screaming, "vinegar" as if it were a deadly
poison.)

Looking back at my Italian family, I see many of their beliefs,
traditions, prejudices, practices, proscriptions, taboos as artifacts of
times long passed. Yet my relatives live so vividly in my memory.
They are with me, in me, are part of me still, alive in how I think
and feel, how I relate to others, how I care for my family. How I
cook and serve food. How I celebrate, how I grieve, how I feel my
place in the world.

This is how I remember them, how I felt while I was growing
up. I make no claim about accuracy. Memories like dreams—set
down as children lived them—without judgments or understandings
of adult perceptions. I was a child, always watching, listening, trying
to understand them—the lovable, sometimes funny, sometimes sad,
always fascinating members of my large family. I offer them to you,
their stories, the lives of first-generation Italian-Americans thriving
alongside the Hudson, a lifetime ago.

Grandpa's Barbershop

I WISH I HAD ASKED MY GRANDFATHER why he came to America. He was a barber, working in a small town near Naples. He had a wife and a son (my Uncle Nick), brothers and sisters, and a large extended family. But he left all that, and with his wife and infant son he came to America.

He must have thought he would prosper, and live out the American dream—and he did do well here. Landed in New York City, then traveled to Newburgh, in upstate New York, where he found work with a barber, Sal Palmieri, who had a busy shop on Broadway.

They had four more children: Aunt Maria, Aunt Bella, Uncle Mike, and my mother, Clara. When my mother was thirteen, her mother died of pneumonia. Grandpa struggled trying to raise five children alone, and when he visited his family in Italy a year later, he met Rosalia, a widow with a young son, Vinnie, whom he brought back to Newburgh to work for him, keeping house and caring for his children. Grandpa and Rosalia married, and in the next few years had two children: my Aunt Angie and my Uncle Danny. These eight children, some with a different mother, one with a different father, made up the family I knew growing up.

When old Mr. Palmieri retired, Grandpa took over the shop and made it his own—playing his opera records from the old country, singing Italian songs, playing his violin and concertina, and hiring his cousins, also barbers, who made their way from the old country with the promise of work at Nick's Barbershop. Eventually, Uncles Nick and Mike became barbers as well, and had jobs waiting for them at the family shop.

Grandpa's barbershop was always full of people—Newburgh Italians who gathered to speak their language, sing their songs, read their newspaper, La Stampa—a daily, saved each week and sent to Grandpa by his sister, who had moved to Turin. And to eat the Italian treats my grandmother baked for them in the apartment upstairs. Later, when Grandpa and Rosalia married, they moved to the house on Robinson Avenue, near Downing Park. Rosalia continued the tradition of home-baked pastries for the customers at Nick's Barbershop. Word spread, and soon there was a steady crowd of men who'd come for haircuts and shaves, and end up staying the afternoon to soak up the atmosphere, listen to the music and sample the latest from Rosalia's kitchen.

I loved going to the barbershop, just to sit and watch the haircuts, listen to the music, the talking, the singing. There would usually be a card game in a corner of the shop, where men could sit in as they waited. And there was Aunt Bella.

Aunt Bella, with her red hair and blue eyes, was strikingly beautiful. Everyone thought so. She worked as a kind of manager—keeping track of who was next, making appointments, collecting the fees for the haircuts and shaves, maintaining records—and she often joined in the singing, providing harmony and contrast with her clear, sweet soprano voice. She enjoyed the admiration and attention she got from the customers. Grandma said she liked the men too much; Aunt Maria said she'd end up in trouble. I could never get a clear explanation of what 'in trouble' meant, but I had the beginning of an understanding when Aunt Bella suddenly got married and soon after had my cousin, Toomie. It was all so sudden and so secret, and everyone acted like they'd been married for a long time. My mother kicked me under the table when, in Grandma's kitchen, I asked when the wedding had been and how come we hadn't been invited to it.

Toomie became the darling of the family, with his curly platinum hair and happy disposition. He looked a lot like his father, my new Uncle Tom. Toomie was actually named after his father, Tom, but Aunt Bella said he was too cute to have a man's name, and decided Toomie suited him better.

At first, no one liked Tom. He was different from anyone in the family. His original sin, the one for which there was no fix, was that he was Polish (Tom Ambrosiak). "Not a real man!" according to Uncle Mike, a rough kind of guy who shouted, no matter what he was saying. Uncle Tom was blond, blue-eyed, much taller than anyone in the family (another unfixable flaw)—and he ate Corn Flakes!

"Corn flakes?! What the hell kind of food is that?" my father asked, when Tom brought a box of it to our house one morning.

"It's good, Jimmy. You should try it," Uncle Tom said, holding up the box. "Look at all the vitamins in it."

"Vitamins? How good could it taste with all that crap in it?" My father believed only Italian food was safe and worth eating.

Little Toomie, who was to stay with my mother for the day, was happily feeding himself one corn flake at a time.

"Let me show you," Uncle Tom said, as he poured some flakes in a bowl, poured milk over them and sliced a banana on top.

"There," he said, putting the bowl before Toomie and starting to feed him. "Wanna try it?"

"Hell, no!" my father said, "Clara made me a real breakfast an hour ago—eggs and ham."

"I'll try it," I said, and got a bowl. I liked Uncle Tom and didn't want him to feel bad. My father frowned his disapproval, as if I'd defected to the enemy—not to Uncle Tom, but to the suspicious and deplorable American food he was always warning us about. But

I discovered: I really liked corn flakes.

Everyone ended up really liking Tom, too. It was impossible not to, and even Grandpa couldn't resist how Uncle Tom fit in at the barbershop. He'd come for a haircut on a Saturday morning and stay the afternoon, playing cards and singing the Italian songs he learned by writing down the lyrics on the back of his magazine and memorizing them. He sang the Italian words with great feeling and enjoyment. But Aunt Bella acted different when Tom was there. She stayed near the cash register, busy with record-keeping, not joining in the singing and joking with the customers, as she did at other times.

"Something's up with that one," my father said, nodding toward my Aunt Bella. Uncle Nick, who was cutting my father's hair, said, "What do you mean, Jimmy?"

Aunt Bella was sitting on a high stool near the cash register, reading a magazine, while Tom was at the small table in the corner, drinking coffee and having a biscotti with one of the regulars.

"I mean, she's not happy. She's got a good husband and a terrific baby and she looks like she'd rather be somewhere else."

Uncle Nick turned to look at her. "Hmm," he said. "That's not good."

Uncle Tom worked for the telephone company and was out of town regularly on business trips. During those times, Aunt Bella would go out to the clubs with her old girlfriends. Aunt Bella loved to dance. She was the best dancer in the family and usually the best dancer wherever she went.

"She's asking for trouble," my mother said, when my father told her how Aunt Bella ignored Uncle Tom at the barbershop. "She doesn't say anything, but I'm pretty sure she's not happy with Tom."

My mother, of all the four sisters, was the one who worried most about everyone in the family. She went on, explaining to my father.

"I asked her what she was doing, going out to clubs with her single girlfriends, and she said, 'Dancing, Clara. What's wrong with dancing?' She was so annoyed that I was asking. We know what that means."

"Well, once again, there's nothing you can do about your sister or your brother, or any of them. No matter how stupid their decisions are, they're all adults. They have to decide which sins they want to commit and then do their penance for them. You know, you gotta pay the fiddler," my father said, chuckling as he picked up the newspaper and looked over the front page.

"Oh, really? What are you, Father Petrillo? Maybe you should assign them their penance."

"Jesus, Clara, I'm trying to help. Don't blame me if your brother and sister are screwing up."

"Who said she's screwing up? All I said was she's asking for trouble."

"Okay, so you didn't say it—so I read between the lines, so I'll stick to the lines from now on. What's for dinner?"

"I don't know what's for dinner. I'm not thinking about dinner. What is this, an all-day diner? What am I, a short-order cook?"

"Holy shit! You're really mad?"

"Yeah! I'm sick of my stupid family screwing up their lives, and you getting such a kick out of it."

He got up. "And I'm sick of your damn stupid family. There's always some kind of bullshit going on and you're always all upset. I'm gonna go sit down and read the paper. Call me when dinner's ready. That is, if the diner isn't closed by then." He walked fast toward the living room, the newspaper under his arm.

My father's anger terrified me. I was always worried it would end up being a horrible fight that lasted all day, with yelling and banging on tables. I usually thought my father was wrong and my mother was right, but this time I thought maybe my mother was really worried about Bella and she was kind of blaming my father. I didn't like the feeling of not being on my mother's side. She needed my help, as he was so much more powerful. It was silent support I offered, since I would never say a word to either of them when they fought. Somehow I believed it helped her that I was on her side, even though she didn't know.

This time felt wrong. I felt like a traitor. I felt sorry for my mother, something I never felt for my father. She was worried about Aunt Bella and now she had my father mad at her. My father, angry, that was a very scary thing.

No one spoke all through dinner. My mother didn't eat at all. I'd whispered to my brother just before he sat down, "Daddy's mad," our way of warning each other: be careful, be quiet, do everything right. "Daddy's mad" meant be ready to duck, if anything at all displeased him.

Holiday Dinner

HOLIDAY DINNER AT MY GRANDPARENTS happened at two separate tables—one for the adults (as many as sixteen of them) and one for the
children (about twelve of us.) The adults sat at a very long table in
the finished part of the basement, while Grandma ran up and down
the stairs serving the many courses that made up the traditional Italian holiday feast: antipasto and soups and salads and macaroni and
meat balls and roasted chickens and stuffed meats and vegetables in
sauces and potatoes in casseroles and pastries and cakes and fruits and
nuts and cheeses. And espresso. Grandma cooked everything herself,
and Grandpa made the wine—although my uncles Nick and Mike
would bring wines they made, to compare with the old man's.

We kids had our own table in the unfinished part of the basement, across the room. We'd have macaroni and meatballs—and
some, but not all, of the grownup dishes.

The food was spectacular, but the most memorable part of this
were the antics of the aunts and uncles. They sat for a whole afternoon, ate and talked and drank wine and laughed and cried and sang
and shouted, in a mix of Italian and English. And fought.

Aunt Maria and Aunt Bella would sit next to each other and
talk softly, at first. No one could tell when the tone began to change.
It always seemed that suddenly they were shouting at each other,
crying and gathering up their plates and glasses and silverware to

move to another place at the table, disrupting other aunts, who had to change places with them. Then they would tell their version of the argument and expect total agreement and support from those nearby, drawing as many as possible into the fray. Aunt Maggie, an aunt by marriage and Irish (!) would sit watching and drinking her wine, and when voices reached a high volume, would point her finger upward and declare that there would be no winner—and did anyone know the song, "Bona Note, Amore?"—and the women would begin to sing in Italian, their beautiful soprano voices in close harmony, all arguments forgotten.

The men had their own stories to tell and arguments to settle. Who made the best wine? Uncle Nick and Uncle Mike were in fierce, perpetual competition for this recognition. Uncle Mike would taste Uncle Nick's wine and sputter, declaring it vinegar. Uncle John, an uncle by marriage—which in this family was the lowest life form—would argue with Uncle Mike, and my father, also an outsider, would join Uncle John in supporting Uncle Nick, while Uncle Vinnie lined up with Uncle Mike.

These altercations, sometimes escalating to the brink of fisticuffs, would never stop until my grandfather pounded his fist on the table and yelled *"Statti zitto!"* which I believe is Italian for "Shut the hell up."

We kids would listen and take sides, with feigned passion and conviction, in imitation of the other elder table.

One of us would say, "Uncle Vinnie is right." Another would disagree, taking Uncle Nick's part, and the kid's table would begin its own drama—our Italians-In-Training exercises—until one of us would pound on the table and yell a Grandpa impression of, "Statti zitto!" which would propel us into uncontrollable laughter, with spit-takes of watered-down grape juice ("fake wine") and much coughing and falling off chairs.

One Easter afternoon after dinner, we who sat at the kid's

table were breaking off the arms and legs of the little cake men
(with colored eggs in their bellies) that my grandmother made for
all the children every Easter, while the adults were about to feast
on ricotta pie and espresso (the kid's version was mostly milk.) The
adults were talking with great excitement about my mother's cousin, Rocco, who was coming later to introduce the girl he'd met in
Italy, and whom he was to marry. An argument broke out between
Aunts Maria and Bella about this woman, about whether she really
liked Rocco or just Rocco's money. Rocco owned a very successful
butcher shop and had bought a large older home in town which he
was having renovated. He was almost forty— an ageing bachelor, not
known for the good looks the other men in the family had inherited.
A forty-year-old bachelor was a sign of family failure and shame.

Something had to be done, so at one of the family dinners
Rocco was urged to go to Italy and find a wife. Letters were written
to relatives there, telling them Rocco was coming and they should
get to work finding a good woman to introduce him to—one able
to appreciate Rocco's good qualities, despite his looks. Rocco was
back and forth to Italy a few times before he announced that he had
found someone and was to be married here, in a few months. And
he was bringing her here today at four o'clock, for coffee and cake.

At exactly four o'clock, there was a knock at the back door
upstairs and then Rocco calling out, "Where is everybody?" Aunts
Maria and Bella stopped arguing.

"Down here," my grandfather answered. "Hey, Rocco, *come
stai?*"

Rocco appeared at the top of the stairs and started down, greet-
ing people as he noticed them. All fighting stopped, all eyes turned
toward him, and as his prospective bride came down a few steps, he
announced, "This is Lianna."

There was a collective gasp, then silence. I was struck dumb.

Lianna was a woman of about twenty-five and I was about ten

at the time and…she was my double! If we'd been the same age, she would have been seen as my identical twin. We looked at each other. Both tables were now buzzing with subdued expressions of shock and something like delight and wonder. But she and I just stood there in silence. She walked toward me and I toward her. We looked at each other close up. She said something in Italian—she spoke no English. I said something like, "You look exactly like me," which Rocco translated. She smiled and touched my face. We pointed at each other and laughed softly. It was astonishing. Yet, there was absolutely nothing to say. I had seen a vision—what I was to be in ten years. I couldn't speak for hours. I placed myself where I could see her, sitting at the adult table. I watched her, studied her, until she and Rocco got up to leave. Then I stood at the foot of the stairs.

Lianna turned to me. She held my face with both her hands and said, *"Molto bella,"* which I knew meant very beautiful. I put my hands on her face in the same way she had and said, *"Molto bella."* We laughed at our joke and she looked into my eyes and said *"Ciao, gemella,"* and hugged me. Halfway up the stairs, she turned, smiled and waved.

I sat on the bottom step, unable to move or speak. How could this be? I thought each person was given her own face. How could another person—an older person from a whole different country, have the same face? My face! Or wait, she had the face first, so I have her face. Was it some sort of mistake? Did God run out of faces? Or does everyone have a twin somewhere? My thoughts were spinning around when my brother came to the steps. "So you got to meet your twin. Now you know how you're going to look. Just about nobody ever gets to do that. What's it like?"

"Scary," I said, without thinking. "Yeah…scary."

Uncle Vinnie's Getting Married
—Not to Penny

My Aunt Maria, dispenser of all family gossip
and news, sounded breathless on the phone: "Tell your mother when
she gets home to call me right away. Your Uncle Vinnie's getting
married and not to Penny!"

Wow, I thought. Not to Penny? But Penny is his girlfriend.
Uncle Vinnie had convinced Aunt Angie to rent her upstairs apartment to Penny so she'd be across the street from my grandmother's,
where he lived. The whole family was shocked when they heard
about Penny moving in. Aunt Angie said she had thought they were
just friends when she agreed to rent to her. But when she saw that
he was always there, until all hours of the night, she realized Uncle
Vinnie had misled her. But by then, it was too late. Besides, Aunt
Angie had grown to like Penny, liked having her upstairs.

When I told my mother the news, she looked stunned, her eyes
and mouth wide, as if she was about to shout out something but it
freeze-dried before she could speak, before she could blink.

Then, finally, "What? Are you sure you heard her right?" I
nodded. "Are you sure that's what Aunt Maria said?" I nodded
again. "Yes. I'm sure. Just call her. She said to call her. You'll see."

"Yeah, well I will, but you…you just go out and get the clothes
off the line. Right now, you hear?" She seemed to think I was re-

sponsible for the bad news.

"Yeah! God! Okay!" I grabbed my jacket and went out, knowing the clothes weren't urgent but that my mother wanted me out of the house, so she could grill Aunt Maria about our wild and shady Uncle Vinnie.

We lived in Beacon, but the rest of my mother's family lived in Newburgh, the town across the river, where all the family stories originated: Uncle Vinnie and his gambling, his girlfriends, his Cadillacs and Vicuna coat, the vacations in Acapulco and Puerto Rico. He had a real estate business, but while he was always on the brink of closing a "big deal," none of them ever went through. He reported so many times that the deal "crapped out just before closing" that the eye-rolls began as soon as he used the term, "big deal." My father always said, "So where does he get his money?"

True to Italian tradition, my Uncle Danny—the other, younger bachelor—also lived with my grandparents. Uncle Danny was Uncle Vinnie's opposite: quiet and moody, a piano-player in late-night bars, who mysteriously disappeared for a week at a time, then reappeared, looking thin, disheveled, and barely speaking for several days. He was so different from everyone in the family. Even his looks: blond hair, light blue eyes, fair skin, much thinner than the other men in the family, and always dressed in dark clothes. He didn't join in the loud talking and laughing and arguing after dinner. He seemed to be looking into the distance, to other places, other things. When the men played their card games and fought over who had made the best wine, Uncle Danny would often quietly move to the parlor and play sad songs on the piano. No one seemed to notice this. Sometimes I would sneak into the parlor, where children weren't allowed, to listen to him play. After a while, he'd look around at me and nod, and continue playing. I think he understood that I liked him, liked his music.

Aunt Angie lived across the hilly street from my grandparents, up three houses from my Aunt Maria. She was married to a very big man, a businessman. He owned a pocketbook factory, had lots of money—and a very quick, scary temper. Every Christmas he gave pocketbooks to all the women in the family. He'd arrive with about twenty pocketbooks in a big box and dump them on the floor for my aunts and older cousins and grandmother to fight over while he stood laughing. Aunt Maria and my mother often talked about him, disagreeing about whether or not he was hitting Aunt Angie. She was the youngest sister and very pretty and sweet. (Or, as Aunt Maria suggested *stonato* which I finally figured out meant, stupid.) My mother would snap at Aunt Maria when she said that. "Innocent, not stupid, Maria," she'd say. "Don't be so mean."

We all liked Uncle Vinnie's girlfriend, Penny. She was lively and smart and pretty, and she made us all laugh at her funny observations. She once said of Great Aunt Rosie, who wore all black for forty-five years after her husband died, "I happen to know that under that black dress, Great Aunt Rosie is wearing a red bra and panties." This, in my grandmother's kitchen, was as disgraceful as it got. My grandmother clucked her tongue and made the sign of the cross, but when she turned to get the coffee from the stove, I caught her secret smile.

Now Uncle Vinnie was marrying some woman nobody knows.

I got the clothes off the line in record time and rushed back in to hear my mother on the phone say: "Oh Maria, no, not her—it can't be her. It must be someone he met on one of his vacations."

(My father always said of Uncle Vinnie's vacations: "Vacation from what?")

My mother went on: "He never took Penny on any of those vacations to Puerto Rico and Acapulco and wherever, so who was he with? You're saying Josephine Penzetta? I can't believe it. She's so… so…I don't know. No, not ugly—not ugly—just plain. You know, no makeup, hair in a bun, dark dress down to her ankles, flat shoes.

What the hell is wrong with her? Yeah, right, what the hell is wrong with him? Okay, maybe a little ugly. She does have that mustache. But yeah, she's nice enough, I guess. I only met her that once, at Angelo's wedding—remember? She sat with her old aunts and uncles and Vinnie was sitting there for a while, talking to one of them."

My mother laughed. "Yeah, ha-ha. Yeah, she must have caught his eye. She caught something— maybe under the table." She laughed again and I could hear Aunt Maria from across the room laughing on the phone. I knew there was some meaning I didn't get, but I couldn't figure out what.

My mother asked, "What did Bella say? She doesn't know? Okay, I'm gonna call her. And how about Angie? She doesn't know either? Oh my God, Angie's gonna have a fit! Okay, you tell her. I'll talk to Bella." The phone rang and rang and conversations filled with shock and disbelief and loud laughter and quiet whispers went on through dinner, and into the night. What an uproar! Everyone seemed mad at Uncle Vinnie. And no one could imagine why he would choose Josephine Penzetta over Penny. (My father said, "Yeah, she's no looker, but how much money does she have?")

The next day, Sunday, everyone was at Grandma and Grandpa's for dinner, as usual. Uncle Vinnie was absent—another "big deal"—and Aunts Bella, Maria, and Angie were in the kitchen with my mother, helping with dinner. Maria, stirring the rigatoni, whispered to Angie, "Did you see her at the wedding? Oh...*molto brutta!*" (which I already knew meant ugly.) Aunt Angie said she didn't remember her but that Aunt Bella had told her she looked old enough to be Vinnie's mother.

I was trying to stay out of sight in the kitchen, curled up in Grandpa's chair in the corner, my head hidden behind an Archie comic book. This was the best stuff since cousin Mario took off for a weekend with a woman he met at the bar where Uncle Vinnie played piano and his wife, Florence, was going to divorce him. My grandfather took him to a room in the attic to "talk some sense into him," and when they came back down, cousin Mario looked like he'd been crying. But Florence didn't divorce him and now they have another baby.

This was better, in a way, because there was a mystery to it: Who is this woman? Does Penny know? Why is he not marrying Penny? Irish Aunt Maggie, the only non-Italian woman married into the family, said, her finger wagging in Aunt Bella's and Aunt Angie's faces, "You shouldn't be gossiping like this. It's a sin. God will make you suffer for it. And it's nobody's business if he marries...what's her name?"

"Josephine. Josephine Penzetta," Aunt Maria offered. "Wait till you meet her. She looks like the old ladies in the pictures of Mama's aunts in Italy.

"Who?" Aunt Maggie's head snapped around. "What'd you say? Did you say Josephine Penzetta? I know her! Her brother's a builder in Balmville. Oh Jesus, Mary, and Joseph! God must've had a migraine when he put that one together—didn't put a single pretty thing on her. God forgive me for sayin' it: she looks like the perpetually sad saints, always lookin' down at her own feet when she walks, poor thing. What's he doin' with her?"

"God will make you suffer for that," Aunt Maria said. Everyone laughed, including Aunt Maggie, on hearing her own words quoted.

My mother, looking worried, said, "We have to get to the bottom of this. Something's fishy. Smells worse than mama's *buccala.*"

The phone calls continued, tapering off by the middle of the next week, until that Friday. On Friday, the phone rang during dinner, a thing that happened only in emergencies. It was Aunt Angie. Mama took the phone to the living-room, stretching the extra-long curly phone wire to its limit, while we continued our dinner in the kitchen. All we could make out from that distance was an occasional exclamation: "Oh no! How awful! How could he!" My father shook his head at that last exclamation and said, "I wouldn't put anything past him."

Mama came back to the kitchen and started clearing the table, not noticing that we hadn't finished eating. "He's bringing her to dinner Sunday. Can you believe it? And poor Penny across the street!"

"Clara, we aren't done here and you haven't even started. What are you doing?"

"Oh," she said, sitting down, "I don't know what the hell I'm doing. How could he be so cruel? And I don't want to meet this person. None of us do. We're going to have to tell him. I just don't know what I'm going to do." She began picking at her food, rapidly pushing potatoes from one part of her plate to another.

"You're pushing your food around," I said, laughing. She often corrected us for that.

"This is not a laughing matter," she said, glaring at me.

"Sorry," I muttered, feeling guilty for upsetting her.

"I don't know what I'm going to do," she said again.

My father sipped his wine. "Nothing. You'll do nothing. We'll show up. We'll meet this woman. We'll mind our business. Let him deal with the mess he's made," my father said, telling my mother in tone and quieting hand gestures, that she should calm down.

"Oh, it's always so easy for you. Because you don't really care about any of these people. What do you care that my brother has lost his mind and is going to bring some dried-up old hag into the family for some reason that can't possibly make any sense. It doesn't matter to you. It's not your family.

"Listen Clara, let's not you and me fight about your brother again, okay? So Vinnie's gone nuts. But what can anybody do? He's your baby brother, but he's thirty-one years old. He's going to do whatever he wants to do. Right? He's *ostinato*—nobody could ever tell him anything…about anything, right?"

"Yeah," she sighed, "I know. I guess you're right. But it's just awful."

By the time Sunday arrived Mama had spent hours on the phone with her sisters, and they made two decisions. One: Aunt Maria, the oldest, would talk to Uncle Vinnie, would ask him to explain why he's made this stupid decision. Two: Aunt Angie, who knew Penny best, would talk to her to find out if she knows about Josephine Penzetta, and how she feels about Uncle Vinnie breaking up with her. The four sisters agreed that these conversations had to be reported by Sunday at noon, so they would be armed with the facts before they were to meet Josephine Penzetta for dinner at one o'clock.

Meeting Josephine

AUNTS MARIA, BELLA, ANGIE AND MY MOTHER met at Grandma's at twelve noon on Sunday, an hour before dinner, as planned. They told Grandma they would set the table and get things ready, but the first item was to talk over what Aunt Maria had learned from interviewing Uncle Vinnie about why he had decided to marry Josephine Penzetta instead of Penny, his girlfriend of three years (and the one the family liked), and what Aunt Angie was able to find out about how much Penny knew about Uncle Vinnie's plan to marry Josephine Penzetta. I could see they were anxious to get to their discussion; their faces were flushed, their movements quick and jerky, their comments interrupting each other as they each took a cup of espresso and a biscotti and started down the stairs to the basement.

They sat facing each other at one end of the long table.

"Okay Maria," my mother said, "what did our stupid-ass brother have to say for himself?"

Aunt Maria stirred her coffee, dunked her biscotti in it, took a bite, and said,

"Well, here's his first story: he wanted an Italian woman. Penny is not Italian."

They all groaned. Aunt Maria went on. "So I said, 'well Penny has never been Italian, but you stayed with her for three years, so that can't be it,' and he said 'well, but I was never going to marry

Penny'—as if everyone should have known that—then I said, 'oh, come on, that's a bullshit story, what's the real story?' and he said, 'well, you know, Josephine has never been married,' and I said, 'so what?' and he said, 'Penny has been married and divorced,' so I asked him why that mattered and he said (are you ready?) he said, in his most innocent voice, 'I wouldn't be able to get married in the Catholic Church'."

Everyone laughed.

"Oh boy. Now suddenly he's a big Catholic," Aunt Angie said.

"Yeah. Saint Vinnie," my mother added.

Aunt Maria continued. "So I told him he didn't seem to worry about the church these three years he was sleeping with Penny. 'But sleeping isn't marrying,' he said."

Aunt Bella, her face red, shouted, "Oh my god, he's just been using Penny and lying to her. What a son-of-a-bitch!"

"No," Aunt Maria broke in, "No, he said he really loved Penny, but he can't marry a woman who's been with another man."

"Oh my God," Aunt Angie said, "what a hypocrite! It doesn't' matter how many women he's been with, but a woman has to be a virgin?!"

"I asked him that," Aunt Maria said, "and he said, 'Yes, it matters when it comes to marriage.'"

"So it's not the church, it's his own idea—he needs to marry a virgin," Aunt Bella said.

Aunt Angie said, "Wait a minute. How does anyone know for sure Josephine is a virgin?"

My mother said, "Really? Who would want her?"

"Mean! That's just mean, Clara," Bella said.

"Yes, but true," Aunt Maria added.

"So that's the whole story—she's a virgin and she's Italian and he's going to marry her, although he loves Penny. Still doesn't make sense." My mother got up from the table. "I don't want any part of this. I'm not going to this phony wedding and I don't want to meet this holy Italian virgin."

"Me neither," Aunt Angie said, "But she's coming to dinner in an hour."

"What did Penny say? You talked to her, right?" Aunt Maria asked.

"Yes, Penny knows he's going to marry Josephine, but she doesn't know why. She's brokenhearted. She said she's going to move out of my apartment as soon as she finds another place. The poor thing." Aunt Angie had tears in her eyes.

My mother had let me come with her to this meeting, after I begged her and promised I'd never tell anyone what happened. But now I didn't want to be there. I had to turn away from the others to hide my eyes, filled with tears. I loved Penny and I was so sorry for her. And now I hated Uncle Vinnie.

"Well, okay, so what are we going to do when she comes," Aunt Bella asked.

There was a long silence.

"Come on, she'll be here in half an hour. What should we do?" she asked again.

"Well, Jimmy said we shouldn't do anything. We should just let him stew in his own juice," my mother said. My father hadn't really said that, but it was probably what he meant.

Aunt Maria said, "I think we shouldn't make it so easy for him to just plop her down in Mama's kitchen with all of us acting like it's perfectly okay."

"No, I don't think we should do that either, but we can't be too mean to her. It's really not her fault." Aunt Angie was always the kindest of all the aunts.

My mother said, "I don't want to let Vinnie off too easy. He's always getting away with murder: debts that Papa paid off, so he wouldn't get his knees broken; all the cars he wrecked; all the bad deals he got into—"

"—that big brother Nick got him out of!"

"—and all the women trying to find him when he'd disappear instead of breaking it off with them—

"—and all the times he left town 'until things cool down'." My mother shook her head. "No! He's got to pay the piper this time. He's been dancing free his whole life."

"Yes," Aunt Bella said, "but what are we going to do today—at dinner—in twenty-five minutes?"

"Okay," mother said, hands flat on the table. "So we'll be civil. Not real friendly, but not nasty either. Just civil."

So it was decided. We all went upstairs to the kitchen, where Uncle Vinnie would come in with his Holy Italian Virgin. The aunts stood around the kitchen table, arguing about where Josephine Penzetta should sit.

"No, not there," Aunt Angie said, "she'd be right next to Papa and that wouldn't be good. How about there, by the china closet, where we can all watch her?"

"Oh, I don't know. Maybe she should be here, close to the door, in case she wants to run away when we give her the cold shoulder," Aunt Maria quipped, laughing.

"Near the china closet is best," Aunt Bella said.

"I'm not going to be that nice," my mother announced, sitting across the table from the designated hot seat.

"Okay. So just don't say anything," Aunt Angie suggested.

"I don't need you to tell me how to act, Angie. I'll do what I want," mother said, glaring at her.

"Okay, okay, Clara, don't get all mad at me. We're all on the same side."

The back door opened just then and in walked Uncle Vinnie, in his camel-hair coat and white scarf, his highly-shined brown shoes, his fresh manicure, his close shave, his perfectly cut hair, and his arm around the plainest, dullest, worst-dressed, worst put-to-gether woman that had ever walked into Grandma's kitchen.

"This is Josephine," Uncle Vinnie announced. "And these are my sisters," he said, pointing as he identified each one. "Clara and her daughter, Maria, Bella and Angie, and my mother, over there, by the stove." Josephine nodded to each, but didn't smile.

My mother whispered something to Aunt Maria, who covered her mouth to giggle.

"Here, Josephine, sit here," Aunt Bella said, giving a warning look to my mother. "Would you like an espresso?"

"Okay," she said, and sat, her black pocketbook on her lap.

Aunt Bella poured coffee into a tiny espresso cup, put it on a matching saucer, added a tiny spoon to the saucer, all done very slowly, deliberately, with exaggerated gracefulness, at which Aunt Maria put her hand over her mouth and giggled.

"Would you like sugar or Anisette?" Aunt Bella asked, shooting a disapproving glance at Aunt Maria.

"A little sugar," Josephine replied in a small voice, "just a little."

She took a bit of sugar with the tiny spoon and stirred it into her coffee.

"Biscotti?" Aunt Angie asked, holding a tray of them before her.

"No thank you," Josephine answered, without a smile.

"Josephine works in the fabric store in Balmville," Uncle Vinnie announced in a too-loud voice.

"Oh, do you like to do needlework?" Aunt Bella asked. Aunt Bella was an excellent seamstress and could embroider, knit, crochet, and even tat, which hardly anyone could.

"No, not really, "

Josephine answered, "I just got this job because my brother's sister-in-law owns the store."

"Oh," Aunt Bella said, in a tone that conveyed: well that's all I've got. Somebody else take over.

"Oh, so you come from Balmville. Our sister-in-law, Maggie, well she was a Gilhooley then, came from there. Did you know her?" Aunt Maria asked.

"No," Josephine replied, and sipped her coffee.

"Josephine's a lot younger than Maggie. She wouldn't know her," Uncle Vinnie said, a note of annoyance in his voice.

"Maybe her older brother knew Maggie. Your brother is older, isn't he?" Aunt Maria turned to Josephine.

"How do you know him?" Uncle Vinnie sounded suspicious.

"I don't know him. I just know of him," Aunt Maria said, with a trace of impatience.

Uncle Vinnie shook his head in disapproval, then turned to Aunt Bella.

"We're going to visit Great-Aunt Philomena after dinner. Josephine made *sfuyadels* to bring," Uncle Vinnie said, sounding like a small boy proud of his new friend.

Aunt Maria, famous for her cooking, asked, "Oh, do you like to cook, Josephine?"

"Not really. But I do bake a little," she answered. "Sometimes."

"What do you like to bake?" Aunt Maria asked.

"Mostly just bread," Josephine said, "and sometimes *sfuyadels* or *cannoli*."

"She makes incredible *cannolis*," Uncle Vinnie said, with exaggerated enthusiasm.

"Oh, I love *cannolis*," Aunt Angie offered, pouring more coffee into Josephine's cup.

"Okay," Grandma said, "let's get moving. Here." She handed a large tray of antipasto to Aunt Bella. "Bring this down. Maria, you get the bread. Angie, is the table all set down there?"

"No, I don't think so."

"Well, you get that ready. And don't forget the kid's table gets the old dishes and glasses. Here, Clara, you take this tray down. You can get the cheeses in the downstairs refrigerator."

My mother told me I could help, and should follow her.

Josephine said, "Can I help?"

"No, no, no," my grandmother said, "you are a guest." Uncle Vinnie said, "Josephine likes to help, Ma. Just give her something to do."

Grandma, understanding the situation, said, "Oh alright, here, Josephine, you can bring these olives and bowls down."

Josephine jumped up from the chair, put her pocketbook on the seat, and took the olives and bowls from Grandma. She looked around to see where to go and seeing my mother leaving the kitchen, followed her. I followed Josephine. She was small—short and thin. She was wearing a very dark blue dress with tiny white dots on it and a blue sweater. She wore pearl earrings and a long silver chain with a crucifix hanging from it. She had no makeup on, but was wearing a little pink lipstick. She wore her hair in a bun, pulled so tightly back that I thought it must have hurt. Her nails were cut short and her shoes were plain black leather, with short heels. She didn't look horrible, but she just wasn't pretty. Not at all. I couldn't help but think of Penny.

My mother went to the refrigerator room for the cheese. Josephine stood at the foot of the stairs, not knowing where to go. It was silent for a moment, then, from an alcove in the basement where the dishes were kept on shelves, Aunt Maria's voice could be heard.

"Jesus, did you get a load of that dress? Where do you even find a dress like that?"

Aunt Bella said, "At the old ladies' home! I don't know what the hell he's doing with her. She looks like Sister Maria Joseph from the fourth grade at St. Mary's."

Aunt Angie, busily setting the table, slammed down a heavy water pitcher, and yelled, "Stop it! God! Why do you have to be so mean? Okay, so we're mad at Vinnie for dumping Penny. But we don't have to take it out on poor Josephine, do we? It's his fault, not hers. I feel sorry for her for getting mixed up with him. Just think what she's in for."

Josephine, who could neither see them nor be seen by them, stood at the foot of the steps. She turned, looked at me, tears in her eyes, and handed me the olives and bowls she had carried downstairs. She said nothing, but ran up the stairs. I put the olives and bowls on a nearby shelf and ran to the room where my mother was unwrapping cheeses for the tray.

"Mom, oh, this is so terrible!" I was crying.

"Mom, Aunt Maria and Aunt Bella were saying mean things about Josephine and she heard them!"

"What? Oh my god. What did they say? What did she do? Where is she?"

"She just ran up the stairs. She was crying."

"Oh, Jesus Christ!" My mother put the tray down and hurried to where my aunts were busily setting up for dinner. I didn't follow her, but started up the stairs, not knowing what I would do once I got there. I heard my mother shouting at them as I closed the cellar door at the top of the stairs.

Josephine was sitting at the table, her eyes full of tears, twisting a handkerchief in her hands. Uncle Vinnie, sitting next to her, was saying: "But something must have happened. You wouldn't be crying for nothing. What happened?"

"Nothing," she said, "I just got confused or something. I don't know. It's all too much. Your family…it…it…it's just all…a lot."

I couldn't believe what I was hearing. She wasn't telling him. Why not?

"Did somebody say something?" he asked.

"No, no, not really. I just…l don't know how…to…to…talk to them."

It was a lie. She was lying to Uncle Vinnie.

"Because I'll set them straight if they said anything," he said, standing up.

"No, no…don't say anything. Nobody said anything. It's just me. I'm just nervous meeting everybody all at once. It's okay. I'll be okay." She dried her eyes with the twisted-up handkerchief. "Just don't say anything. I don't want to make trouble."

She noticed I was standing near her. She looked at me. Her eyes told me not to say what happened. I sat down next to her and told her with my eyes that I wouldn't.

Grandma came to the table with a cup of latte and placed it in front of Josephine. She looked up with a small smile, whispered, "Thank you." Grandma, not comfortable with gratitude, went back to her cooking.

"Hey, where's mine?" Uncle Vinnie said, half-kidding.

"Hey, help yourself, Vinnie. You're a big boy now," Grandma said over her shoulder, as she took a chicken out of the oven.

Josephine smiled for the first time. For a moment, she looked almost pretty.

Second Childhood

Grandma's house smelled like Sunday.

The aroma of sauce set to simmer on the stove before sunrise, the meatballs and sausages added hours ago. Stuffed chickens roasting in the oversized oven, along with trays of roasting vegetables, and two ricotta pies. All blended with the lingering fragrance of fresh-baked, crusty Italian bread.

One Sunday morning we arrived at Grandma's kitchen earlier than usual, so my father could install an additional lock on the back door—one Great-grandma would not be able to reach, even if she stood on a chair. She had often dragged chairs to the pantry, the china closet, and the top shelf in the coat closet in the front hall, for hats. Climbing up on them created the kind of havoc that would make her mother chase her around the house, wielding a wooden spoon. Great-grandma would scurry around, laughing, knowing Grandma would never be able to catch her.

"Come over here, Grandma, and stand on this chair," my father said, making it sound like a game. He guided her to the back door and helped her stand on the chair, encouraging her to reach up as high as she could. She was into the game and did what he asked. He marked the door at her fingertips. Then he thanked her, told her she did a good job, and quickly installed a simple sliding lock a few inches higher than the mark.

A few days before, Great-grandma had let herself out the back door at five am and up-ended Grandpa's tomato garden, laughing as she dug a deep hole. Her long blue cotton nightgown tucked into her rolled-up stockings, her long white hair flying freely around her head as she sang an Italian work song she'd learned as a child. A young couple had moved into the house next door and the man, returning from his morning run, phoned Grandma to warn her that her mother was into some new mischief in the back yard.

It hadn't taken long for the nice young couple to catch on to her antics. On the day they moved in, Great-grandma had escaped through the back door, walked into their kitchen, and began un-packing their pots and pans, placing them in the refrigerator, the stove, the cabinets, the pantry. The young woman screamed at the sight of a perfect stranger in her kitchen. Grandma, who had real-ized her mother was missing and was out looking for her, heard the scream and approached the neighbor's open back door and found Great-grandma grinning among the pots and pans, and the horrified young woman, backing away. Grandma tried to apologize in her broken English, explaining that Great-grandma was 94 years old and into her second childhood.

She was exactly my height when I was ten years old, and acted like a child half my age. She ran around the dinner table, poking adults in the back, then, pursued by an Aunt or Uncle, ducked behind the living-room chairs and sofa, then scampered up the attic stairs to her bedroom. Part of the attic was hers, part Uncle Danny's and part used for stored furniture, luggage, and racks of clothes, which were great hiding places. Her giggle would give away her location but her quick moves saved her from capture long enough for the pursuer to wear out and give up the chase, admitting they wouldn't have known what to do if they had caught her.

My brother and I just loved Great-grandma, as did all our cousins. But our parents furrowed their brows when they heard of her antics, muttered "tsk-tsk," rolled their eyes and shook their heads. We called her "Nonna," Italian for "grandmother" when we spoke of her, but she insisted we call her by her name, "Angie". Grandma and my Aunts thought it disrespectful, so we compromised by calling her "Anginonna," which outsiders considered a "lovely name," but which my oldest cousin, Nick, thought sounded like a fatal disease.

We loved the Anginonna stories that Aunt Maria, who lived across the street from Grandma's, was always ready to tell. When Aunt Maria arrived on this particular Sunday, she told us what later became known as, "The Little People Knots Story."

According to Aunt Maria, about a month ago, Anginonna began telling stories about the "little people" who lived under the floorboards in the corners of the attic and came out only at night. Grandma paid scant attention, dismissing them as make-believe tales her mother made up for attention. Anginonna was insulted by this, insisted the little people were real, and would stomp up to her attic room and sulk. After a while, she'd forget what she was sulking about and return to the hub of Grandma's house, the kitchen, back to her usual jovial mood.

One morning, Anginonna appeared in the kitchen and sat down before her breakfast of toasted Italian bread and jelly and strong black coffee mixed with heavy cream and started to add the many teaspoons of sugar she loved so much. Grandma, washing dishes, her back to Anginonna, warned her about too much sugar, and turning to check, took one look at Anginonna, dropped the cup she was holding, and began screaming. Anginonna's pure white hair, grown very long during the eight years she wouldn't allow anyone to cut it, was every bit of it, tied in tiny knots. Anginonna claimed to remember nothing, but believed the little people, angry because Grandma didn't believe in them, had done it while she was asleep. Grandma called Aunt Maria to come help her untie the many knots. When

Aunt Maria saw them, she suggested they just cut them all off, leaving her practically bald. Anginonna, hearing this, began to cry.

"It would serve her right," Aunt Maria said, "for doing such a stupid thing and then lying about it, blaming it on those made-up little people."

But Grandma couldn't do that to her mother, so they spent most of the day untying the "little-people knots," repeating again and again what a bad thing it was that Anginonna had done.

After the telling of the Little-People-Knots story, the rest of the family began to arrive for dinner and as the story spread among the aunts and uncles and cousins, it passed into the collected Anginonna Archives—the stories of Great-grandma's antic-filled Second Childhood.

Later that night, on the ferry home to Beacon, I asked my mother, "Mom, does everybody have a second childhood?"

"No," she answered, "not everyone—not like Great-grandma's second childhood. Some people just get old and can't remember anything."

"I hope I get one," I said. I was looking out the window at the stars. We had been first in the line of cars to drive on to the ferry, which put us where we could see the river and the sky. The moon was full and very low that night. I could see it reflected in the river.

I was thinking of Anginonna, wondering what she was like when she was young. Was she like my mother? Like me? I was wondering if she remembered who she used to be before she started her second childhood when I noticed my father was unusually quiet. I asked him if he wanted to have a second childhood. He took a long time to answer. I thought he was going to ignore my question, but then he cleared his throat and said,

"No. I don't think so. The first one was bad enough."

"Why? Why was it so bad?" I had never heard that before.

"Because…oh, lots of reasons…I'll tell you some other time." I didn't think he would.

"How about you, Mom? Do you want a second childhood?

"Oh, I don't know," she sighed, "I'll let you know when the time comes." It sounded like she'd have a choice. She hardly ever answered questions about herself, so I figured this was her way of not answering.

"How about you, Johnny?" I asked my brother, who was two years older.

"A second childhood! Are you nuts? I don't even want this one!"

Johnny was always wanting to be older—to move out, see the world—and get away from our father. Our father was never very nice to Johnny.

"But maybe your second childhood would be better than this one," I said without thinking, without considering what my mother and father might feel.

"Well, I've had enough second-childhood talk for today," my father said.

He turned the radio on, at first to loud static, then to quiet music. I stared at the moon reflected in the water, and the sky full of stars. Across the river a long train with its lighted windows hurried to unknown places, and in the distance the warning light on the mountain top lit up the clouds over Beacon—the other world, where we lived.

Aunt Maria

MY MOTHER AND HER SISTERS always seemed so strong, so in control of their lives. So ready to tell a good story, a juicy bit of gossip, a comic incident. Whenever I could, I found a way to listen, unbeknownst to them. I would sit on the steps, behind a wall, or hide behind a book, as if deeply involved in my reading or homework. Sometimes I would be in the room, having "fallen asleep" in a chair—quite convincingly, I guess, since they would continue their stories, without cleaning them up for the kid in the room.

One Sunday evening, after dinner at Grandma and Grandpa's, Aunt Maria invited all the women to her house just across the street for a dessert she'd made, while the men stayed behind, to play cards. Grandma was tired, so it was just the four sisters and me. I said I had to read a book for school, and sat in the big chair in the living room, facing the archway to the dining room, where they sat with their coffee and rum-soaked vanilla-cream cake. I expected some good stories so I settled in, ears perked up for some gossip, or ribald tales of uncles or cousins, my face hidden behind my Social Studies textbook.

Aunt Maria began talking about the house next door to Grandma's. She said she was thinking of buying it.

"Why?" my mother asked. "You haven't even been in this house for a year. Why would you want to move so soon?"

"Yeah," Aunt Bella added. "This is the third time you've

moved in two years. What's wrong with this house?"

"Well I don't like it here anymore. I don't like the people next door and I hate the kitchen—it's too small."

"But Maria, it's so much work to move. You have to sell your house and pack all this stuff. God, aren't you tired of doing all that?" Aunt Angie looked at my mother and shrugged her confusion.

"I'm tired of a lot of things," Aunt Maria said, "but I can't change them. The only thing I can do is move."

"What do you mean, Maria? What are you tired of?" my mother asked. "You have everything—all the best furniture, all the best clothes, expensive jewelry, and…"

Aunt Maria interrupted, "Yes, and what, Clara? Do I have a husband I chose myself? Do I have a child?"

I was shocked to hear Aunt Maria sounding unhappy. She was always so full of laughter and funny stories. I peeked over my book and saw that her eyes were full of tears.

"Oh God, Maria," my mother said, "No, you don't. You don't have those things. Oh my god, so this is why you're always moving? But does it help, Mare? Does it help at all?

"A little—for a little while. But then I look at him. He falls asleep right after dinner every night. He hardly ever talks. He's not a bad man; he's just old. He was always old—and I'm not. I should have fought Papa when he brought him home for me. Such an old man—he was forty-two. But I was too afraid. I was only seventeen. You know, Clara, you were there. Papa thought he'd be a good husband. He had money. He had a good job on the railroad— he was a supervisor. And he didn't have any bad habits." She tapped the rim of her cup. "But he didn't have any good habits either. I found that out later. I should have fought Papa."

"And I should have fought for you," my mother said, "like I did later when he brought home that old guy from the Torsini Funeral Parlor for me." She had tears in her eyes.

Aunt Bella stood up, "Holy Christ! This stinks! There's got to be a better answer than moving every two years. "You can move in with me, Maria," Aunt Angie said, "and just leave him. You're still young. You'll meet someone else." She was crying.

"Oh, he'd die. He's sixty-five now. What's he gonna do? No, I'm stuck." Aunt Maria sipped her coffee. "My only move is to move."

A few weeks after that night, Aunt Maria announced she'd bought the house next door to Grandma and Grandpa's and would move in two weeks. We were at the Sunday dinner table, with all my aunts and uncles seated there and all the cousins at the kid's table nearby.

"What the hell's wrong with you, Maria? You're always moving," Uncle Nick said.

"You don't have to help this time, Nick," Aunt Maria said, "I'm just telling you."

"It's not about helping—Jesus, Maria—but what's the matter with you, are you..."

"Nothing's the matter with her," Aunt Bella interrupted. "Nothing you have to know, Nick, nothing you'd ever understand—and you don't have to be such a 'stadoonze' either."

Vinnie, in a sing-song, teasing voice said, "Maybe Maria just wants to be closer to mama and papa."

"Oh yeah, Vinnie, you of all people should talk," my mother said, "Thirty-one years old, still living with your mommy and daddy. You got some nerve talking about anybody else..."

"Hey! I was just joking. Jeez!"

"Okay, let's not have a free-for-all over this," Aunt Maggie, the peacemaker, said, "So Maria is going to move. Who else's business is it but hers?"

Uncle Mike chimed in, "How about her husband's—right? Where is he, Maria?"

"He went to his cousin, Fanny's. Her porch step just collapsed with her on it and she sprained her ankle."

Vinnie and Nick both laughed at that.

"I wish I could have seen her break that step. Fat Fanny breaking the house down—that must have been a sight to see." Uncle Mike snickered.

"Yeah—Fat Fanny!" Uncle Vinnie added, as if announcing a new service: "'If you need your house demolished, call Fat Fanny!' Remember how she broke the chair when she sat in it last Thanksgiving? It took three of us to get her back on her feet." Wicked laughter from the men.

Aunt Angie stood up and shouted, "Shut up, you *chooch animales,* she's a human being. Not everybody's perfect like you two jailbirds. At least Fanny doesn't get arrested for illegal gambling in the back of the pool hall."

There was a stunned silence for a moment, while Aunt Angie wiped the tears she couldn't hold back and sat back down. She was unaccustomed to confronting her brothers and they were unaccustomed to hearing her express a strong opinion. She kept her eyes downcast for several minutes, until the conversation resumed, in a different direction.

"I'll help you out, Maria ," Uncle Vinnie said.

"Yeah, so will I. I just don't get it. But I'll still be there," Uncle Nick said.

"Me too," Uncle Mike added. "We'll all help. Don't worry."

When I was able to see Aunt Maria's face, I could see that she had been crying, too.

When Aunt Maria revealed how unhappy she'd been all the years she was married to Uncle John, how sorry she was that she hadn't fought my grandfather when he brought Uncle John home to marry her, all three of them cried. It surprised me to see them cry for Aunt Maria. I always knew they loved each other, but I never realized that meant they would suffer for each other.

A few years before, my mother had told me that when their mother died Aunt Maria (the oldest girl) started taking care of the rest of them. When their father went to Italy and came back with a new mother for them, all the sisters were angry at the way the new mother took over and bossed them all around, including Maria.

When Grandpa brought Uncle John to meet her, she didn't really like him, but agreed to marry him, mostly because she was afraid to disobey her father. But also because she could get away from the stepmother, who had singled her out for more punishments than the others. Aunt Maria had always loved to dance and sing, to laugh with friends, so whenever Uncle John was on one of his frequent work trips, she would go to the local clubs with her single friends and Aunt Angie's husband's cousin, Fanny. Aunt Angie said it was to be expected that one of those times she would meet a man who would like her—someone her age—someone she would have chosen if she'd had a choice when she was young. And it happened: she met Bob. At first it was just someone to dance with, joke with, sing with. But before long, Bob was who she'd look for and plan to meet, and who she'd spend the whole time with. Fanny looked the other way, but knew what was happening. Aunt Maria was falling for the guy and he for her, and there was nothing anyone could do or wanted to do to stop it.

"What the hell are you going to do, Maria?" my mother asked her one afternoon at our kitchen table.

"I don't know, Clara. I just don't know. But it's the first time in my life I've ever been happy. The only time."

"You'll have to leave John, won't you?"

"Oh, how can I do that? I'm afraid. He doesn't know how to take care of himself and he has no one but me, now that his brother died. He's never been mean to me for a single minute in all these years. He's not a bad man. I don't know how I could do that to him."

My mother's eyes were full of tears. She went to the stove for the coffee pot, poured more into Aunt Maria's cup, then her own.

"I don't know how I could do that to him."

My mother put her hand over Aunt Maria's on the table, and patted it.

"I know, Maria. I know," she said.

And they sipped their coffee.

An Italian Easter Story

SOME TIME DURING GREAT-GRANDMA'S NINETY-FOUR YEARS, through a slow, imperceptible process, she split into two very distinct personalities. A spritely imp in her second childhood, ready for mischief and childish fun—and another, a suspicious, sulking, wounded victim, sure that everyone was out to get her, punish her, blame her for everything. Sometimes these personalities would flip from one to the other without warning, with no apparent cause. When this shift occurred, from imp to victim, she would gather the children around her and plot against the family adults, not in the spirit of fun, but with the goal of revenge for some imagined wrong-doing against her. As children we weren't aware when Anginonna was not in fun mode, but out for vengeance. We would go along with whatever, believing it was all a game. We didn't know how far Anginonna was willing to go, when she felt seriously wronged.

On Easter Sunday, when I was ten, Anginonna sat and ate at the children's table with all of us cousins, as we had our Easter Dinner—antipasto, leg of lamb, spaghetti pie, roasted vegetables, rice and sausage pie, salads—and for dessert, Easter bread and ricotta pie. Each child got a little cake bunny with a colored egg in its belly, instead of adult desserts. Anginonna, muttering *"non 'e giusto!"* (not fair), chose her moment and, crouching down from her four-foot-two height so she was barely visible, made her way to the adult table, stole one of the ricotta pies, and served it to all of us at the kid's table. Since Grandma had made three of them, no one noticed at first. But Aunt Angie came by to check on her two young sons, and seeing the empty pie tin, asked, "What is this doing here?" Grandma shrieked and started after Anginonna, waving a *moppine* (dish towel), swatting at her all the way up the stairs. She came back a few minutes later, and told us that we musn't go up to Nonna's room because she was being punished. We all thought it was very funny that someone ninety-four years old could still get punished.

After dessert the Aunts did the dishes in the big basement sinks, singing Hit Parade songs as they washed, dried and put away the dishes, platters, and bowls. Then we all went upstairs, where the men were playing cards in the dining room. The women gathered in the kitchen for demitasse and anisette. Some of us kids went out to the front porch to play board games and some to the back yard to play ball. After a while, when we gathered in the kitchen, we asked: Was she still punished? Could we go up to her attic room to see her?

"Okay," Grandma said, "You can go up now."

So we hurried up the attic steps to Anginonna's room, calling to her on the way. But she didn't greet us. We rushed in to her attic bedroom, calling her name. But she was in her bed, covers up to her chin, hands folded over her chest, eyes closed, not moving.

"Anginonna, you can get up now. You can come downstairs, Grandma said so."

"Come on, wake up, Anginonna. Wake up."

But she didn't wake up. Didn't stir at all. We lifted her hand. It fell back, limp.

"No!" We screamed. "She's dead!"

We scrambled down the stairs, yelling that Anginonna was dead. My mother, Aunts Maria, Bella and Angie and Grandma ran to the attic steps and hurried up to Anginonna's room. We kids all followed. My grandmother went to Anginonna's bedside.

"Mama," she said, "Wake up, Mama! Wake up!" Aunt Bella said, "See if she's breathing."

Grandma put her ear to Anginonna's face and shook her head. "No."

"Maria, what are you doing?" my mother asked.

"Trying to find her pulse," she said, holding Anginonna's wrist. "Where is it supposed to be?"

Grandma was crying, "Oh Mama, *e culpa mia, e culpa mia.* It's my fault, my fault. I chased her up the stairs. I yelled at her for the pie. I hit her with the *moppine.* It's my fault. She knelt at her mother's bedside, crying. *Scusa, scusa,* Mama.

Aunt Maria began to cry, then Aunt Bella. My mother said, "We should call the doctor. We don't know what to do."

Aunt Maria said she knew the doctor, so they went downstairs to make the call. Grandma was crying hysterically, begging for forgiveness, praying for Anginonna to wake up. Aunt Bella, standing behind her, embraced Grandma and pulled her up. Grandma fell into her arms, sobbing.

"Mama," Aunt Bella said, "Come, you have to lie down or you're going to collapse. Don't worry, we'll take care of her. Come on, now." She and Aunt Angie led her to the stairs, She could barely walk. They helped her down the stairs.

Some of us kids were crying. No one could speak. We stood there, staring at Anginonna's dead body, crying, praying.

"Hey! I think she moved!" Nicky, the oldest cousin said it in a loud whisper. "I think her hand moved."

We moved in closer, all together.

"She's trying to say something," my brother said.

We leaned in even closer. Her eyes were still closed and she didn't move.

"Anginonna, are you awake?" I whispered in her ear.

"Shh," she whispered. "No worry. Gramma no dead."

Shh, shh," she put her finger over her lips. "Gramma no dead. No tell. Shh! Shh! Shh!"

"Oh, she's playing dead," my brother said. "She wants everyone to think she's dead— why?"

"Are you kidding? It's the greatest trick of all—playing dead," my cousin Nick said. "What an incredible prank. They're all down there going nuts." He laughed.

"Shh! Shh! Shh!" she said again.

We heard Grandma from downstairs crying out, "Tell Papa, go tell Papa." The men, playing cards in the other part of the house, hadn't heard what was happening. But in a few minutes we heard them on the attic stairs.

My Uncle Nick, arriving first, shouted, "You kids get out of the way. Give Grandpa enough room."

Grandpa, a barber, had the reputation of knowing a lot about the human body, as was expected of barbers in those days. We all moved back from the bed. Grandpa arrived, followed by Uncles Vinnie, Danny, Mike, and my father.

Grandpa looked at Anginonna, took her hand, held her wrist. He leaned down, put his ear to her chest, his hand at her neck. He stood upright; studied her face.

"What is it Papa?" Uncle Vinnie asked.

"Is she cold?" my father asked.

"Is she breathing?" Uncle Mike asked.

Uncle Nick said, "Leave him alone. He has to think." Two of my Aunts, Angie and Maria, had come to the attic room to hear Grandpa's opinion.

"We called Father Petterosso," Aunt Angie said to Uncle Nick.

Grandpa turned and moved slowly through the crowd that had gathered, holding his arms out in front of him to clear the way. Slowly, silently, he went down the steps, everyone following. He arrived at the kitchen, stopped, and facing the crowd, announced, very quietly and calmly: "Grandma—is—not—dead."

There was a hush, then a buzz of questions, which Grandpa stopped with one raised hand.

"She may be in a coma, might be faking, but not dead."

There was a flurry of happy reactions, then questions: what should they do?

"First," Grandpa announced, "No one goes up there until we decide."

Everyone agreed.

"Now we make a plan."

Grandpa explained that he believed she was faking. In fact, he was sure. Some of the kids nodded.

"So here's the plan," he said, and everyone gathered around the table.

The women sat in chairs, the men stood behind them, we kids squeezed in where we could. Grandpa stood in his place at the head of the table. He looked at each of his children, their spouses, and all of the grandchildren.

"Okay," he said, "Grandma is pretending to be dead. You ask why, but we know why. She feels she has been treated badly, that she isn't respected, isn't important. She was punished—and she's telling us we better watch out, because she can punish us as well. Look at Mama (my grandmother), she is very upset. She feels very bad that her mother is so hurt that she's playing dead. So how do we put an end to this?" He raised his eyebrows. "Well, we could just wait. Eventually, she'll have to get up. To eat—use the bathroom— something. But that isn't the right ending for Grandma's important message."

"But what can we do?" Aunt Maria asked.

Grandpa spoke in a serious voice. "Well, Grandma is a special woman. She has lived a very long time and taken care of a lot of us. We owe her a special response. This is our chance to give her one."

"What do you mean, Papa? How can we do that," my mother asked.

"We can have a funeral—a wake." He said.

Exclamations all around: "What?" "That's crazy!" "Oh my God!"

Then my father said, "Wait a minute. Let's find out what he means."

"Thank you, Jimmy," Grandpa said. "Here's what I mean. We gather around Grandma's bed, very seriously, acting like she's dead. We tell her, in her native language, how sorry we are that she won't be with us anymore. We tell her how lucky we've been to have had her with us for so long. Not everyone speaks, we should choose. Bella, you're a big talker, you should speak. Vinnie, you're the smooth talker, so you should speak. Nick, you're the oldest, so you too—and Maria, you live next door and know her best, you can speak. The rest of us should say something too, but short—like 'Goodbye Grandma. I'll miss you,' or something like that. And all the kids can say their 'goodbyes' as well. Let her know she is important, respected. That's what I think we should do."

After more discussion of what to say and who will say it, and a bit of practice, everyone was ready. Grandpa took Aunt Bella aside for a few minutes and whispered something. Then Grandma and Grandpa led the way up the attic steps to Anginonna's room. The four adult speakers stood closest to her bed; Grandma and Grandpa stood with them. The rest of us stood behind them, circling her bed.

Grandpa spoke first: "Mama, we have all come to say goodbye and to tell you how much you have done for all of us and how sorry we are that you will not be with us anymore. Rest in Peace, Mama Angelina."

Aunt Maria spoke next: "Grandma, I am so sad that you have gone from us. I will miss you every day and remember you always. You taught me all I know about cooking. You were the best cook

I ever knew. You taught me that cooking is a beautiful thing to do, that feeding people is giving them love. I will miss you until one day I will see you in Heaven."

Uncle Nick said: "Grandma, I will always remember how you took care of me when I was a child. You taught me prayers and you took me to Mass and you made sure I learned Italian, so I would always know what everyone was saying. You read me stories in Italian and that made it easier to learn. And you made the best meat balls in the world. I will miss you, Grandma, but I will see you in Heaven."

Uncle Vinnie spoke next: "Grandma, you will always live in my memory as the most fun Grandma ever. You told me funny stories and taught me funny songs and you showed me how to play pranks on people to make them laugh. Whenever I felt bad, you were the person I looked for to make me feel better, and you always did. Goodbye Grandma. I'll miss you."

Aunt Bella spoke last: "Oh Grandma, you were always the best Grandma that ever could be. You taught me to sew. You were such a great dressmaker. I learned to make beautiful dresses from you. And you taught me to have patience. You had so much patience when I was trying to learn sewing and knitting and crocheting. I'm so grateful to you. And I'm so sorry you have left us before your ninety-fifth birthday next month. We had such a beautiful party planned. All our relatives were planning to come—the aunts and uncles and cousins we haven't seen in a long time—they were all coming to celebrate your wonderful ninety-fifth birthday. But now that will be a sad day for all of us. So goodbye, Grandma, God bless you. We all love you."

Aunts Maria, Angie and my mother were whispering during these lines about the birthday:

What? What the hell is she talking about? What party? There's no party!

The others began to move up to her bed, saying goodbye and

how they would miss her, each mentioning the ninety-fifth birthday party. Everyone was talking about the party, who was coming, the big birthday cake, and how it was too bad and so sad that Grandma would not be there.

Suddenly she sat up and shouted, "Gramma no dead! Gramma back from dead! Gramma no dead!"

"Ohh!" Grandpa shouted, "An Easter Miracle! She has come back from the dead! Like Christ! She has risen!"

There was much cheering and clapping and everyone hugged Anginonna and each other.

My mother whispered to Aunt Maria:

"Wonderful idea, the birthday party. Of course now we're gonna have to do it."

Aunt Bella whispered back to my mother: "It was Papa's idea."

Aunt Bella

MY MOTHER STOOD AT MY BEDROOM DOORWAY. "Come on, get ready, we're going to Newburgh."

"How come, mom? Why today?"

"I have to see your Aunt Bella. Come on now, I have to get back here to fix dinner."

"Okay. But why are you in such a hurry?" I looked for my sandals.

"I can't explain right now. But I want you to come with me. I don't like to ride on the ferry alone."

So we hurried to the bus stop and made it just in time for the eleven am boat. My mother took a magazine out of her pocketbook as soon as we sat down and began leafing through it.

"Look at this," she said, pointing to an ad for home perma-nents. "I'm going to try one of these next week. Tessie is going to help me."

I liked Tessie. She was somehow distantly related to us, but I never could remember how—something like the cousin of my aunt's cousin. She was younger than my mother and very stylish. I loved her laugh—it sounded like Woody Woodpecker. And she was always doing terrific things with her hair. She reminded me of Uncle Vin-nie's old girlfriend, Penny—her clothes, her hair, her makeup—and she was funny, like Penny. I missed her but whenever I asked about

Penny everyone would say they didn't know where she moved to, and never heard from her. I was afraid she had died of a broken heart and nobody wanted to tell me. My mother said that people don't really die from a broken heart. They just feel terribly sad. But I still believed they could because I read about it in one of my mother's romance stories.

My mother wouldn't let me stand on the outside deck of the ferry, where most of the young people stood, so I looked over her shoulder at the magazine she was reading, and tried to follow the story about a young girl madly in love with a pilot, who she thought had another girlfriend in another country. My mother loved romance magazines and romance radio programs. She listened to one I could never figure out, "Portia Faces Life." Was it Portia Face's Life?—About the life of a woman named Portia Face? Or was it about a person called Portia facing her life? Then there was "Just Plain Bill," which had strange music playing in the background, and "Stella Dallas," some fancy woman having all sorts of romantic troubles. My mother listened to these and other stories while she dusted and ironed and folded laundry. She always looked happy when she was listening to the radio stories. I used to watch her and think how much I dreaded growing up and having to listen to those stories and do housework. I wanted to be a detective. Or an opera singer. Or a writer. Or a spy. Not a housewife!

We arrived at the Newburgh Ferry Station and found a bus to Renwick Street, where my Aunt Bella lived with Uncle Tom and Toomie.

"Now when we get there, I want you to play with Toomie or go into the living room and…here, you can read my magazine. Or read something else, or turn on the radio. I just need to have a private conversation with Aunt Bella. And I don't want you to listen and interrupt. Okay? I'm sorry. But this is important. So can you do that?"

"Okay. But I'll need a drink first. I'm really thirsty." I wasn't looking forward to this visit at all.

Aunt Bella looked shocked when she opened the door and saw my mother standing there.

"Clara! What are you doing here? I didn't know you were coming. What's the matter?"

My mother, pushing me ahead of her said, "Well, can we come in?"

"Of course. And how are you, Sweetie?" Aunt Bella said to me and kissed my forehead.

"I'm really thirsty," I said. "I mean, Hi, Aunt Bella."

"I have some orange soda. How would that be?" She smiled at me. "Come on, sit down."

She poured me a glass of orange soda and put an ice cube in it.

"What do you want to drink, Clara?"

"I don't want anything. I have to talk to you about something...private." She nodded her head toward me.

"Oh?" Aunt Bella said. "What about?"

"It's private!"

"Okay, well, let her take the soda to the living room. It's okay. Toomie is taking his nap."

I took my soda to the living room and chose a chair where I knew I could see them at the table. My mother sat down at the head of the table. Aunt Bella sat near her.

"What is it, Clara? What brings you across the river to have a private talk that we couldn't have on the phone?"

She paused. "I know, Bella."

"What are you talking about, Clara? What is it that you think you know?"

"I know about the guy, whatshisname—Denzel Holesaddle? Whatever. I know about him. Is that his real name?"

"Not exactly. So what is it you know, Clara? What's got you so upset?"

"What the hell are you doing, Bella? I can't believe what I'm hearing. What are you planning to do?

"What is it you think you know?" Aunt Bella asked.

"That you are leaving Tom and running away with this guy, Denzel. That's what I know."

"And how do you know that?"

"Never mind how, I just know it. Is it true?"

"Suppose it is? Are you here to talk me out of it?"

"Shouldn't I be? Have you gone crazy? Why would you do such an insane thing?"

"I know." Bella closed her eyes, shook her head. "It does sound crazy. Maybe I am crazy."

"But why? Who is this guy? How long have you known this guy? What's this all about?"

"I can't explain it. I don't know what to say. I can't help it. It's…just…he's in the service, stationed at Stewart. He's being discharged…and…he's leaving…next week, to go back home. To West Virginia."

"Oh, Bella. This is crazy. You mean you're thinking of going with him, just leaving Tom? How about Toomie?"

"Oh I know, Clara." She covered her face with her hands. "I know it's crazy. I just can't help it." She looked up at my mother. "I feel like I've never been alive before. Like all this time with Tom— he's a good guy, I know—and I've been trying to be in love with him. But I'm not. I never have been. I made a terrible mistake that one time and then there was no choice. I had to marry him. Papa almost killed him and I knew I had no choice" Her lip quivered.

"I've tried to be happy. I never looked for anyone else, Clara. Suddenly he was just there, and I feel like I can't let him go." She looked away from my mother. "I never knew what this was like, never knew what it was like to love somebody like this—so much that I'll do anything to be with him. I can't let him go, Clara. I've never been alive before. I feel like I'll die without him. We knew it the first time we met. He feels the same way. Everything about him is what I need. I'm happy just standing next to him. I know it will be awful for Tom. But he deserves to be with someone who loves him like I love Denzel. And he'll find that when I'm gone."

"But what about Toomie?" My mother's voice was softer, pleading.

"Oh I couldn't take Toomie from Tom. That would kill him. And he's a better father than I'm a mother. He's a better person— don't think I don't know that. No, Toomie stays with Tom. It will kill me but I couldn't do that to Tom or to Toomie. He'll have a good life with Tom.

"Oh, Bella. You're making the biggest mistake of your life. I'm so afraid for you. West Virginia is a long way from here. Aren't you worried? And how will you see Toomie? How will he be without his mother? God, have you really made up your mind?"

"Yes. There's nothing else I can do."

"Yes, there is, Bella. You can stay. You'll forget about Denzel. You can have a decent life with Toomie and Tom. He's a good guy and he loves you so much. Anyone can see that."

"I don't have a moment of happiness with him. I never want to be close to him. I dread it when he comes home from work. He wants to kiss me so I dream up all sorts of things I have to do at that very minute. I don't want to hear about his day. Or sit and have dinner with him. I don't want to go to bed with him. But I don't want to hurt him either. I spend my life pretending. I'm twenty-four years old—should I spend the next 50 years pretending? I didn't choose Tom any more than Clara chose John. You don't understand. You chose Jimmy. However it is now, he was your choice. You can't even imagine what it's like to live your life with someone you didn't choose. Someone you don't love, someone you don't want to touch you. Oh God!" She sobbed.

My mother had tears in her eyes. "I didn't know it was this bad, Bella. Why didn't you tell me?"

"I was trying to do it. I was hoping it would get better—that I could fall in love with him. But instead, it got harder. I didn't want to tell anyone. I was pregnant and was supposed to be in love or how else do you explain why you're pregnant? Could I say I had too much to drink? And I didn't realize the chance I was taking, and was never in love with Tom? What would that make me?"

"Just a kid who made a mistake. That's all."

"Not to Papa."

"Yeah. Not to Papa. Oh, Bella. I don't want you to go so far away."

"I know. I'll miss you—all of you. But I have to be where he is. That's the only thing I'm sure of." She put her head down on the table and sobbed again.

My mother took Aunt Bella's hand in hers.

"It's okay, Bell." She used to call her "Bell" when she was a baby.

"It's okay."

I moved from where I could be seen so they wouldn't see me crying.

What Aunt Bella didn't know was that this was just the first step in her sisters' attempts to stop her from what they believed would be the biggest mistake of her life—running away to West Virginia with Denzel Holesapple.

A meeting was called by Aunt Maria, a call to all the sisters and sisters-in-law to meet and make plans to dissuade Aunt Bella. A secret meeting in our home in Beacon, so Aunt Bella would not find out. Aunts Maria, Angie, Connie, and Maggie, and my mother, met in our kitchen on the Tuesday night before Aunt Bella was to leave, on Friday. They had just days to take action.

After hours of disagreement, debate and discussion, they

reached an agreement. They would gather at Aunt Maria's the next day and, since none of them drove, would walk the two blocks to Aunt Bella's house on Renwick Street. They would each tell Aunt Bella what they think about her plan and how they believe it will affect Toomie and Tom and the rest of the family, and ultimately Aunt Bella herself. They each chose a particular aspect of the situation to focus on. My mother had already expressed her opinions to Aunt Bella, and chose to repeat her misgivings about leaving three-year-old Toomie without a mother. I convinced my mother to let me come, telling her I could play with Toomie while they talked, so he wouldn't have to hear them talk about his father, and how they all felt about Aunt Bella leaving him without a mother.

Aunt Bella knew, the moment she saw all six of us at her door, that her sisters had banded together to convince her to change her mind. She closed her eyes and shook her head.

"This isn't going to work." she said, "But come in. I'll put on some coffee."

They gathered around the table, giving Toomie the new toys they had gotten for him, each one talking to him for a few moments. Then I took him to the living room and we began to play. I could still hear what was happening in the kitchen from where Toomie and I settled in the living room, but Toomie was totally focused on playing and not interested in grownups.

Aunt Bella stood at the sink, preparing the coffee pot, talking about Cousin Fanny, Aunt Angie's cousin-in-law, and how she won the Lindy contest at the Roundabout Bar last weekend.

Aunt Maria interrupted her, "Sit down, Bella."

"What? I'm getting the coffee ready, Maria."

"We don't need any coffee, Bella. We've come to talk."

"Why? Why all together like this?"

Aunt Maggie and Aunt Angie rolled their eyes and looked at Maria, so she would speak first. "You know very well why we're here, Bella. Because of what you're about to do," Aunt Maria said.

Aunt Bella, arms akimbo, said, "What difference does it make to you?"

Just then Toomie ran into the kitchen to my mother, showing her a little puzzle he had completed. She picked him up and held him in her lap.

"What difference does it make to him is more the point," she said.

I ran into the kitchen and took Toomie back to the living room.

Aunt Angie said, "How could you even think of leaving him?"

Aunt Connie added, "You'll never live it down."

"I won't have to live it down. I'll be in West Virginia and I won't give a damn what anyone here is saying about me."

Aunt Maggie, the Irish sister-in-law with seven children, said, "How will he ever get over the fact that his mother left him?"

"How would he ever get over the fact that his mother took him from his father, if I took him with me?"

Maria looked around the table. This wasn't what they planned.

"Isn't anyone going to tell her what we're all thinking?" There was a hush.

Aunt Maria continued. "Why the hell would you leave Tom, your wonderful husband and father, to run off with Denzel Hole-sapple, a miner from West Virginia you met a few weeks ago? Have you gone nuts?"

"Maybe. But I love him like I never loved Tom. You, of all people, should understand that, Maria. Could you imagine what you would you do if you met somebody you could love? Wouldn't you leave John? Can't you at least understand this? Can't any of you understand this?"

Aunt Maria looked down and said nothing. Only my mother and I knew how much she was holding back—how hard it was for her to stay with Uncle John when she loved another man. None of the others knew.

"We understand being crazy about some guy. We've all been there. But running away, leaving your child? That I can't understand." My mother began to cry. "He's just a baby."

"How do you think Tom will be able to go on if you do this?" Aunt Angie said, "How will he take care of Toomie all alone? What are you thinking?"

"His sisters will help. They all love him. Tom has to know I don't have the right feelings for him. Anyway, I'm writing him a letter. I don't want to—I'm not doing this to hurt him. Here, let me read it to you."

She took a folded-up piece of paper from her apron pocket. "I'm not finished yet, but I'm telling him…here's the first part:

> In the beginning everyone in my family loved you so much that I thought I could love you too and I was having your baby so neither of us really had a choice. You're the best man I've ever known and nothing I'm doing is your fault. I'm leaving Toomie with you because let's face it you're a better father than I am a mother and I could never take Toomie from you. I love you, Tom but not as I should. Not as a wife should. With me away you'll find another woman who will love you as you should be loved and as you deserve to be loved.

"I'm not finished with it yet. Do you see? This is not something I'm doing in a crazy way. I just can't live like this. I feel like a dead person. Please, understand."

"God help you," Aunt Connie said, "You're doing a very bad thing to your little boy."

Aunt Angie said, "I can understand you wanting to leave but look, if you leave, you take your child and stay where he can see his father. You don't leave your baby and run far away, with another man."

"I do understand, Bella. Really I do," Aunt Maria said, "but you can't. No matter how much you want to, you can't. It's just wrong."

"I understand, too, Bella," my mother said, "and I know how hard this is, but this is a terrible mistake. You'll always be sorry and Toomie will always be hurt."

"No, nobody understands. I don't feel like it's even a choice. I have to be with Denzel. I have to."

My mother was geting angry. "Okay, be with him. Leave Tom, but have Denzel stay here with you and Toomie. Why do you have to go to West Virginia? Why are you the one to move? Why not him?"

"Oh God," Aunt Bella said, "I can't stay here. Can you imagine Papa if I did that? Everyone would hate me. I'd be kicked out of the family. And they would all hate Denzel—Nick and Mike and Vinnie—they'd want to kill him."

"Maybe. But it would all cool down," Aunt Maggie, said. "And when this thing with this guy cools down—which it will, believe me—you'll realize what a stupid and selfish thing you've done. And it will be too late."

Everyone looked at Aunt Bella. She turned her back to them and busied herself at the sink.

"Okay. Let's go," my mother said. "There's nothing more to say. You'll do what you want, Bella. You always have. If you ever change your mind and regret what you've done, let me know. I'll help you to get out of it, if that's what you want. I can't agree with what you're doing, but I want you to stay in touch. Will you do that?"

"Yes. Of course I'll stay in touch. I'm not leaving all of you. I'm leaving Tom."

We all gathered our things. Aunt Bella picked up Toomie and held him. We kissed him and said goodbye. We left in silence, no one knowing what to say.

As we walked down the street, all of us crying, I turned around and saw Aunt Bella in the doorway, wiping her eyes. I gave her a little wave; she waved back. So did Toomie.

The next afternoon, Thursday, my mother called Aunt Bella. I had been home from school a while and was reading in my bedroom when I heard her on the phone. I put my book down and went to the steps to listen.

"Oh Bell," she said, "Please change your mind. Tell him he will have to live here with you so your son will have both his parents. Don't you think he cares enough about you to do that?"

She was crying. I wanted to go to her, but I didn't want her to know I'd been listening, and I thought she wouldn't say all she wanted to say with me there.

"Yes, I know that. But is coal mining all he can do? Can't he find another line of work? There are other jobs here. Don't listen to him, Bell, he just doesn't want to make the effort to find another way."

There was a long silence while my mother listened. Then she blew her nose and spoke in a different, harder tone.

"Well it sounds to me like you aren't even trying to get him to change his mind. Like you really WANT to go to West Virginia without your baby. Maybe you just want to leave your whole life behind, to start a new life without a child to take care of. Maybe Denzit or Dorzel or whatever the hell his name is doesn't want a baby to support, to get in the way. Maybe he's the bum everyone thinks he is. Doesn't sound like much of a man to me, Bella, stealing a man's wife and getting her to leave her child. You don't know what you're getting yourself into. You just want to escape!"

She got angrier and angrier as she spoke.

"Well, you go right ahead and hang up, Bella. If that's your answer to everything I'm saying. But you are going to be one sorry woman when you wake up from this fairy tale you're living. I'm sorry for you. Really I am. Because you don't know what the hell you're doing. Okay. Say goodbye, Bella, but I'm mad as hell at you right now. I'll always help you, Bell, don't forget that. If you should ever want to come back, I'll always help you."

I was so glad my mother said that at the end. She had said such angry things to Aunt Bella. But she let her know, before they hung up, that she would be there if she needed her. That she still loved her.

When I got home from school the next day, my aunts were at our kitchen table. They all had red eyes. Aunt Bella had left that morning. Had taken Toomie to Uncle Tom's sisters and left him there. Got into Denzel's car and drove off.

Later, after dinner, my mother called Uncle Tom. She said he could barely speak. He said that Bella had left him—left a note on the kitchen table, left her wedding ring there, too. And he was going to his sisters to pick up Toomie.

My mother got off the phone, and saying nothing, went to her bedroom didn't come out all the rest of the evening. My father said we shouldn't worry, that she was just very upset about Aunt Bella leaving and she would be alright. But I was worried. Before I went to bed, I knocked on her door. She didn't answer, but I said, "Good-night, Mom. I love you."

"Yes," she said, "I know, honey. I love you, too. Come on in."

She opened the door, stood looking at me for a moment, held out her arms. The tears that had been filling my eyes for the past hour began to flow, and in a moment we were holding each other, both crying.

"Are you going to be alright?"

"Yes, I will be. Don't worry. I'm just so upset that your Aunt Bella has actually left. I kept hoping she'd change her mind." She sat on the bed, patting her tears with a lacy handkerchief. "Here..." She handed me a tissue from the box on her nightstand.

"I don't understand any of this, Mom."

"I know. Nobody does."

"But why did she have to leave? How could she leave little Toomie?" I started crying again.

"It's hard to understand the things women do sometimes when they feel they can't live without a certain man. They seem to lose their minds and they make terrible decisions."

"Oh God! Will I do things like that when I get older? Did you?"

"No, I didn't. Because I married your father when I was young. I was lucky, because he was who I wanted to marry. Bella married a man she didn't love and so she was never happy. She let others choose him for her. That will never happen to you. I would never let it happen."

"But why did she do that?"

She sighed. "She thought she didn't have a choice."

"But couldn't she have just said 'No, I don't want to get married?'"

"Well, I-I'll have to explain that another time, when you're older. It's hard to understand. But I want you to have a different kind of life—where you make decisions on your own, without some man telling you who you should be, what you should do."

"But will Aunt Bella be happy now? After she left her baby and everyone in her family?"

"I don't know. I don't think she realizes how much she'll miss everything she has. Some women just never get to be happy. They try to get the things they want—they lose the good things they had."

Uncle Danny

UNCLE DANNY WAS THE BABY OF MY MOTHER'S ITALIAN FAMILY: four sisters, four brothers. When I first became aware of them, of their importance in my mother's life, I realized that all but two of them had spouses, so the count was not eight, but fourteen. Six couples, and two unmarrieds—"The Bachelors." And there were twelve children, my cousins. I considered myself amazingly lucky to have so many playmates for Sunday Dinners at my grandparent's house.

Uncle Danny, the youngest of all, and one of the two bachelors, was the mysterious one. He played piano on weekends at a club in Newburgh, where my mother's family lived, and worked in a factory during the week, a job he would never talk about. He was different from the other men in the family— quiet, reserved, distant. He never joined the loud arguments and debates the men would have, sitting at the dining room table playing cards and drinking homemade wine. Wouldn't even show up for Sunday dinner, sometimes. But when he did, he would either disappear to his room while the men gathered upstairs, or he would slip out of the dining room during their after-dinner card game and make his way to the parlor, to play the piano—soft, sweet-sounding songs, some familiar, some completely strange, all so sadly beautiful.

At about ten or eleven, I decided Uncle Danny was a lonely, broken-hearted man, who had lost the one and only woman he

would ever love. I was fascinated by this mysterious man and convinced of my romantic explanation. One Sunday, without warning and just before dinner was served, Uncle Danny showed up.
He came down the cellar stairs to where the long table was set for
dinner, where the aunts and uncles were chattering about the nosey
neighbors and the horrible, vinegary wine someone had brought and
the awful dress their cousin Stella had worn to Mass that morning,
when suddenly Uncle Danny arrived—with a woman! A first.

He went right to his usual place at the table, the woman following. Unfolding an extra chair, he made room by motioning for
Uncle Mike to shove over.

Silence. All eyes on Uncle Danny and the mystery woman.

"This is Philomena. I call her Phillie," was all be said, as he
pulled out her chair.

The whispering sounded like hundreds of buzzing bees.

Phillie was dark, certainly much darker than Uncle Danny,
who was blond, blue-eyed and fair-skinned, like Grandpa. She had
lots of curly black hair, like a movie star. She wore a dress tight on
the top and full at the bottom—black, with red flowers all over it,
and black shiny shoes with very high, skinny heels and open toes,
which showed her red-painted toenails. She smiled at everyone, but
didn't speak. I loved that she had a red flower in her hair. She looked
so pretty.

Uncle Mike, sitting next to her, said, "So Phillie. Can I call ya
Phillie?"

"Yes," she smiled, "Of course. Everyone does."

"So Phillie," he continued, "Where did you come from?"

"Well, from Portugal, a long time ago, when I was about eight.
But I've been living in Warwick ever since."

"Oh, so that's a Portuguese accent you've got," Uncle Mike said.

"I don't have an accent. Do I?" She turned to Uncle Danny.

"No, you don't. But Mike there, my brother, now he's the
one with the accent. He speaks with a *Stupido* accent."

When Phillie turned to look at Uncle Mike, Uncle Danny gave Uncle Mike the Italian hand gesture that says, "What the hell are you doing?"

"What!" Uncle Mike says. "What's wrong with noticing she has an accent? It sounded Spanish to me, so I asked, so shoot me!"

"Good idea. But later. Not at the table."

Phillie laughed at that, as Uncle Danny poured wine in Uncle Mike's glass, saluted him and gulped it down. Then he filled his own glass and handed it to Phillie, who took a sip.

"Oh, this is so good," she said.

"Grazie, Philomena," Uncle Mike said, as he bowed. "I made it myself."

"Mmmm," she said, taking another sip. "It's just a little sweet, but not too much."

"It's the grape. It's all in the grape. The grape has to be just so ripe, but not too ripe, or it's all sugar. You know? It's always about the—"

"—yeah, he's a real grape expert, that's why we call him, 'Mike the Grape.'"

Phillie looked at Mike and laughed, "Mike the Grape— that's so silly."

"Yeah, ya think? You know what we call him?" Mike said, smiling.

"Watch it…" Uncle Danny said.

"We call him 'Danny Hot Dog.'"

"You do?" Phillie said, laughing. "Why?"

Uncle Danny sat looking straight ahead with squinted eyes, nodding head. Like he was plotting revenge.

"Well," Uncle Mike started, paused, continued, "No, I think I should let my little brother tell you why."

And so Phillie was introduced to the Patrino family inner sanctum, where all the men had a name with a title: 'Mike the Grape' 'Nicky Numbers' 'Vinnie Vicuna' 'Danny Hot Dog.' And my grandfather was 'Papa the Pope.' Even the brothers-in-law didn't escape the tradition. There was my father, 'Jimmy Tomato,' and Uncles 'John the Train,' 'Freddie Big Bucks,' and 'Tommy Stilts.'

We kids had our own version of the titles. We called our cousins 'Joey Marbles,' 'Nicky Meatballs,' 'Dickie Foureyes,' 'Bobby the Brain.'

In our peculiar family, it was an honor to be given a title. Not everyone got one, and until a man or boy was given a title, he was considered on probation, not yet fully accepted as a member of the Patrinos. Of course, there was no such designation for women and girls. Females were bella or brutta, beautiful or ugly. Nothing else mattered.

Phillie was definitely bella. That was easy to see. What wasn't easy to see was what made Uncle Danny like her enough to bring her to Sunday dinner.

After that, Uncle Danny brought Phillie to dinner every week. At first the aunts found fault with her. Criticized her appearance, accused her of "overdressing," until Aunt Angie said,

"You know, maybe we're missing something. Maybe to us it's just the usual family Sunday dinner, but to Phillie, it's really a date with Danny that she's dressing up for."

The aunts looked stunned. How could Angie, the youngest sister, know something they hadn't thought of first? Yes, of course, Danny was dating Phillie, and she was dressing up for him.

"How cute!" Aunt Maria said. "Imagine dressing up for little Hot Dog." Chuckles, smirks.

Aunt Angie said, "Well, he may be little Hot Dog to us, but I think he's Big Salami to her."

Everyone laughed and said things like, "Oh no!" "Don't make me think of that," and "No, he's the baby." After that conversation, the aunts changed their attitude about Phillie. They began to compliment her on her pretty clothes, her amazing shoes, and her lovely hairdos (which, by the way, were different every week.) Actually,

Phillie was a beautician. She worked in a shop with several other beauticians, and Phillie explained that every week, each of them would get a new hairdo by whichever of them had free time, and they could each get a pedicure, or a manicure. The owner of the shop insisted that each of them be perfectly groomed and coiffed when at work, so he encouraged the pro bono services they gave each other. I had a secret wish to spend an afternoon at the beauty shop, getting a new hairdo and a manicure, and having my toenails painted red.

But I had learned what my father thought of such things on a day last summer when I came home from my friend Linda's, with red fingernails. He had a fit. "Clara!" he yelled out the window to my mother, who was pulling laundry from the clothesline, "Why do you let her go around with that blond girl, that *putttana* who paints her nails? Now look at her. Did you see what she did to her fingers?"

Then he turned to me, "You go wash that stuff off your hands right now."

My mother, rushing up the stairs, dropped her basket of laundry and shouted,

"Jimmy! Leave her alone! She can't wash it off. You need a special remover to get it off. And her friend, Linda, is a nice girl. Don't you call her that. What's wrong with you, using language like that in front of your ten-year-old daughter?"

So much for my secret wish. I figured Phillie's beauty shop would have to wait for at least ten years.

In the meantime, I enjoyed Sunday dinners more than ever. Phillie showed up each week in a beautiful dress, a beautiful hairdo, and an ever-changing rainbow of nail polish. I also noticed that Uncle Danny seemed different since Phillie was with him. He talked more, laughed more, and he even started wearing colors, instead of all-black. After dinner, as the men dealt the cards, and the women cleaned up, Uncle Danny would play the parlor piano as usual but the songs weren't sad anymore. Some were lively and happy. An

Uncle Danny I had never seen before.

This went on for almost three months until one Sunday Uncle Danny and Phillie didn't show up. I asked my aunts why, but no one knew. Grandma said that he had not been home for three days. Before Phillie, Uncle Danny used to disappear regularly, usually for several days at a time. No one ever knew where he went, where he had been, why he had disappeared, and his only answer, when asked, was, "Just around…"

But this time was different. Everyone looked a little worried, and no one said "Oh it's just Danny. He'll be back."

Uncle Danny did come back, but not with Phillie, and he didn't come to Sunday dinner any more. When anyone asked where she was, Uncle Danny would shrug his shoulders, as if he had no idea what happened, and walk away. He went back to being quiet, disappearing Uncle Danny, hardly speaking, rarely smiling, playing those sad songs. Even more quiet now, and the songs were sadder. I felt so sorry for him. I figured out that Phillie had left him, and tried to imagine why. They had such fun together—always laughing and talking to each other. I had begun to imagine their wedding, hoping Phillie might ask me to be a bridesmaid. Imagined the gown I would wear—and I planned to ask Phillie if I could get my hair done at her beauty shop. I thought an upsweep would be pretty with my gown, which would be strapless and pale blue, my favorite color. And I thought my father would let me paint my nails, since it would be for the wedding, after all. I knew I was doing what my mother called "getting ahead of yourself," but it was such fun imagining it.

But now there was no more Phillie. I missed her. Sunday dinners seemed so boring now, without Phillie, and without Uncle Vinnie's old girlfriend Penny, too. I began to wonder: what was wrong with this family? Why did we keep losing beautiful women? Would Uncle Danny suddenly show up with some dopey-looking old lady to marry, like Uncle Vinnie's Josephine? Is that the only kind of woman my two bachelor uncles wanted to marry? I knew I was having mean thoughts, but I was angry and sad and I couldn't help thinking there was something wrong with my uncles, maybe with my whole family.

After a sad, quiet Sunday dinner, while everyone was sipping coffee and eating *struffoli* and *sfuyadels,* my Aunt Maria took an envelope from her purse and said,

"Listen. Everyone, listen. I got a letter from Bella."

"Oh my God, Maria, when did you get it?" Aunt Angie asked.

"Yeah, how come you didn't mention it on the phone yesterday?" my mother asked.

Uncle Nick said, "So what did she have to say for herself, running away with that *barbone* Dozel or whatever the hell he calls himself?"

"You gonna read it or what?" my father said, tapping his fingers on the table.

"Yes," Aunt Maria said, "If you can all be quiet and give me a chance."

"So, go!" Uncle Nick said, holding his hands out for quiet.

"Okay." Aunt Maria took the letter out of the envelope and unfolded it.

> Dear Mama and Papa and Maria, Clara, Angie, Maggie and Connie and all my brothers and brothers-in-law,
>
> I know you are all mad at me and don't understand what I did. Sometimes I don't understand myself. But some of you know how unhappy I've been for years with Tom. Anyway, I can't explain it, and it's done now, so there's no point in going over it again and again. I'm writing to let you know where I am, here in West Virginia. It's so different from Newburgh—kind of dingy and dark. I'm living in Denzel's mother's house. She stays with her sister since Denzel's father died. The house is okay. I hate the furniture, but at least everything we need is here.
>
> Denzel works long hours in the mines and comes home grey

with coal dust. It's kind of funny just this greyish black face with those bright blue eyes and big white teeth. Makes me smile every day when I see him. But I smile. I don't run away like I did with Tom.

I miss all of you, especially on Sunday, when I know you are all together having Sunday Dinner. I can actually smell Mama's sauce. But more than anyone or anything I miss my little Toomie. Every morning when I first wake up I think Oh, I have to get Toomie's breakfast. But then I remember and I cry for my sweet little Toomie. I pray he's happy with his father and his Aunts taking care of him. I hope he gets to visit you at some Sunday dinners.

One day I may be able to come for a visit. Except for Maria and Clara, I don't think I would be welcome. I guess there's no way to be really happy. I'm with the man I love now, but I'm far away from my family and my heart breaks for my little boy.

I miss all of you, especially my sisters and Mama and Papa.

I hope you are all healthy and doing okay. It would be so good to hear from you.

Love, Bella

Aunt Maria folded the letter and tucked it into the envelope. A tear fell, blurring the return address written in its corner.

When I looked around the table, I saw all my Aunts were crying, and so were Uncle Nick and, surprisingly, Uncle Vinnie. My grandfather was wiping away his tears with the great white handkerchief he always carried in his jacket pocket. Some uncles looked straight ahead and said nothing. I thought that after Aunt Maria read the letter there would be a lot of talk about it, but no one said a word. Everyone just sat there in silence. Aunt Angie picked up her little boy and held him on her lap. Uncle Nick put his arm around Aunt Maggie, and Uncle Mike poured more coffee into Aunt Connie's cup. My father handed my mother his handkerchief.

Soon the men got up and went upstairs to play cards, the women started clearing the table. We kids went outside to play.

After that sad Sunday dinner, as my father drove down Broadway to the Beacon Ferry, I asked my mother if she was mad at Aunt Bella for going away.

"No," she said. "I just miss her and I wish she had stayed with Toomie."

"You mean with Uncle Tom?" I asked.

"Well, no. She wasn't happy with him."

"But why? And Uncle Danny and Phillie—why didn't they stay together? And Uncle Vinnie and Penny? How come people are happy with each other and then they stop being happy together and they break up? I don't understand. And why can't we ever see Phillie anymore? I still like her—don't you?"

"Yes. Of course. But…well, it just doesn't work that way. I don't really know why Uncle Danny and Phillie broke up, but you know, he's not like other men. He's had other girlfriends, but they never stick with him. I think it's because he's so moody."

"What does that mean?"

"Well, it means changing from one mood to another. Uncle Danny's moods change so suddenly. He seems perfectly okay one minute, and then the next be very sad. And when he's sad he wants to be alone. Goes to his room or outside somewhere, to be alone. He can sit perfectly still for a long time, just staring, not talking to anyone. We understand that he comes out of it after a while, but other people just can't handle it."

"Oh. Poor Uncle Danny. But why is he so sad?"

"Nobody knows. We've all tried to find out, but he never says." She looked away, took my father's handkerchief from her purse, and dabbed at her eyes. She didn't say any more.

When all the cars were in and the ferry started, I asked if I could stand on the deck for the trip across the river. I always asked, though I knew I wouldn't be allowed. This time, my mother said, "Yes. I think I'll go with you. It's such a beautiful night."

So my mother, my brother and I stood on the deck as we crossed the river. With the wind blowing in our faces, the sky so crowded with stars they seemed to go on forever, the bright moon reflected in the water, and my mother, one arm around each of us—it seemed a perfect world. But when I looked at my mother, tears were running down her face.

"Mom, why are you crying?" I asked.

"Because it's so beautiful," she said, "and I'm so lucky to be here with the two of you."

The next day when I got home from school, my mother was stirring the soup on the old-fashioned stove in our kitchen. She was talking on the phone while she stirred; I don't think she realized she was doing it. I could tell from the way she was talking it was Aunt Maria.

"But you can't say that kind of thing to Danny," she said.

"I'll tell you what he'll do. He'll walk away or just stop talking. He hates those questions."

She was upset. I could tell by how fast she stirred the soup.

"Well, I didn't say I know what to do, I just know what not to do. He's been like this since he was twelve. He never tells anyone anything."

When I dipped a spoon into the soup to taste it, she realized what she'd been doing and stopped stirring.

"Okay, so I'll ask him to come here. Yeah, tomorrow, his day off. I don't know how I'll get him here; I'll make up some excuse. I don't know! I'll think of something. Oh yeah, I know, it has to be me. Hm? Maybe it's because I don't ask the questions he hates."

I was glad my mother would be talking to Uncle Danny because I thought he might tell her what happened with Phillie.

I hoped he'd arrive late enough for me to be home from school. When I got home and saw his car in front of the house, I hurried up the stairs, opened the door, and found them standing there in the hallway.

"So there's no way any kind of piano could ever fit through this small space and make a turn to get into the hallway," he said, folding up his measuring tape. "Why don't you think about a different, smaller instrument?"

My mother nodded while Uncle Danny named string instruments we could try. She didn't have to tell me not to say anything. She had used the excuse that she needed his opinion about there being some kind of piano we could fit through the doorway. My brother, who was not in on the act, blurted out, "What piano? I'm not playing any piano. Who wants a piano?"

"Never mind," my mother said, "We're thinking about something else for your sister to play."

"Oh my god," I muttered.

After Uncle Danny left, my mother called Aunt Maria. "No, Maria, not much. You know how he is: one-word answers. When I asked, 'So Danny, should we be expecting Phillie to show up one of these Sundays?' His answer was,'No.' That's it. One word, no story to go with it. The next question would normally be 'What happened?' but I could see from the way he turned his head away and stared out the window he wasn't going to talk about it. "

"Yup, and when I said, 'After Vinnie gets married in a few months you'll be the last bachelor in the family," and all he said was, 'Yeah, that's my claim to fame—the last bachelor. You can put it on my gravestone: Here lies the Last Bachelor: Danny Hot Dog.' Yeah Maria, you can laugh, but Danny wasn't laughing. It gave me the creeps."

We quickly forgot about the whole topic of an instrument that would fit through the doorway. But Uncle Danny did not. The next Sunday, Uncle Danny led me to the parlor and happily handed me the violin that had been Grandpa's before he got a better one from his brother in Italy. So now, because my mother told a lie to get Uncle Danny to come to our house so she could find out what happened to his girlfriend, Phillie, now I would have to learn to play the violin. He started right away to show me how to hold it and the bow, and Grandpa, hearing terrible sounds coming from the parlor as he sat in the dining room playing cards, joined us in the parlor and took over the violin lesson. At the end of the lesson, he declared himself my violin teacher and decided I would have a lesson every Sunday after dinner. I was to practice half an hour a day every day and in a year, I'd be a pretty decent violinist. I couldn't speak. I wanted to cry.

I wanted to tell Grandpa my mother was the one who should have to play the violin, how she should have to take the lessons. But he looked so thrilled that one of his grandchildren would play his instrument. I just couldn't disappoint him.

And so my life as a violinist began. I imagined myself playing in a concert hall and one day, famous for my playing, being interviewed for the newspaper about how I got started playing the violin. I would answer, loudly: "MY MOTHER TOLD A BIG FAT LIE AND THAT'S WHY I HAVE TO PLAY THE VIOLIN FOR THE REST OF MY LIFE."

As I came out of the parlor, carrying the battered violin case, my mother sidled up to me and whispered in my ear, "I'm sorry, honey. I'll get you out of this. Don't worry."

But she didn't get me out of it. Instead she made up a story and told it to anyone who'd listen, about how the piano (that never existed) wouldn't fit through the doorway, so my daughter had to play the violin and isn't it wonderful, she's so good at it. See how 'fate stepped in' and put the violin, just the perfect instrument, 'right in her hands'?

My mother had lost her mind! There was no other way to explain this. She knew the truth, but there were times when she told that story to relatives and strangers, that I think she really believed it.

"Mom," I would say when the strangers were gone, "You do know that there was no piano and I never wanted to play one, even if we had one, and I certainly never wanted to play the violin. None of that story is true!'

"Oh, well that's maybe how it started out, but it's true now."

"What! What's true?"

"Well, it's almost true. A piano really couldn't fit through the doorway."

What could I say? Maybe she was right. Maybe it did happen the way she told it. Maybe there was a piano that didn't fit through the doorway. Maybe I do want to play the violin. Maybe I'm the one who's crazy.

So I practiced every day, half an hour, and every Sunday Grandpa taught me—all about the violin—its history—how it all began in Italy (which I had doubted, but recently found actually to be true)—how the way you hold it and the bow is the key to getting the right sound. He told me about the great music written just for the violin that only the violin can play. In the beginning, I dreaded the lessons, but after a while, I began to look forward to my time with Grandpa—alone in the parlor, just the two of us with our violins and Grandpa's stories of the old country and his family of musicians and singers, and the festivals and parades and concerts in the streets. Sometimes he would sing for me the songs he and his sisters sang as children. I can't say I ever grew to love the violin, but I did grow to love my Grandpa's stories and songs and the special time I had with him. When I'd come out of the parlor after my lessons, my brother and my cousins would tell me they felt sorry for me for being forced to learn to play the violin. I'd look down and say, "Yeah, it's awful." But secretly I felt lucky and special and a little bit less angry with my mother for setting me up.

Aunt Maria's Move

ONE SUNDAY MORNING, while we were getting ready to go to Newburgh for dinner, we got a phone call from a very excited Aunt Maria. I answered the phone.

"What's your mother doing?" She sounded like she'd been running.

"She's frosting her cake for Grandma's," I said. "You want to speak to her?" I hoped it was good news. "Mom!" I called out. "It's Aunt Maria."

"Go finish the cake, "she said, handing me the frosting spatula and pulling the long curly telephone cord to the living room.

My father was in the kitchen, reading the Sunday paper, drinking his tea.

"What's going on over there?" he asked. "It's always something."

I told him I didn't know but that Aunt Maria was pretty excited about something.

I finished frosting the cake and brought it to the living room for my mother's approval. She was laughing as she said good-bye to Aunt Maria.

"Okay, Maria. I'll see you later. We'll talk about it then. We'll see what everyone else thinks. Yeah, it certainly is cheaper, I'll give you that."

"What, Mom? What's going on with Aunt Maria?"

"You'll see later on," she said.

My father came in with his newspaper. "It's always something with your Aunt Maria," he said, settling into his chair. "Nothing surprises me when it comes to your mother's sisters." He flipped through the paper, looking for something.

"Okay Jimmy, just because you have boring brothers, you don't have to make fun of my sisters."

"Well, you're right. They're certainly not boring. At least we can say that," he said, finding the story he'd been looking for in the paper.

My mother picked up a small pillow from the sofa as she crossed the room and dropped it on my father's head on her way to the kitchen. He calmly took it off and went on reading his newspaper. "Your mother gets huffy about her sisters," he said, chuckling.

When we arrived at my grandparent's, Aunt Maria was sitting at the kitchen table, stuffing mushrooms.

"What kind of stuffing did Mama make?" my mother asked. She grabbed a spoon and tried to dip into it. Aunt Maria pushed it out of her reach.

"Sausage, and keep your paws out of it."

My mother placed the cake she'd made on a cake plate.

"Ohh! Is that your orange cake?" Aunt Maria asked, taking a tiny bit of the frosting on her finger.

"Yeah, and keep your paws off of it, Maria." She gave Aunt Maria's hand a little slap.

I laughed at this. They were so much like my brother and me, in spite of their ages.

"So, what do you think?" Aunt Maria asked.

"Oh, I don't know, Maria," my mother said. "Let's see what Maggie and Angie say. And whose gonna do it? It'll be a big job. You expect to get it done today?"

"What?" I asked, my curiosity growing by the minute.

"Never mind. You'll find out later. Why don't you go help Grandma set things up downstairs?"

"Oh!" I whined, "Why can't you just tell me what's going on?"

Just then Grandma came back upstairs to check on her chickens roasting in the oven, and Aunts Angie and Maggie came in, with cousins Dukey and Freddie. My brother, who had been listening to the ball game on the dining room radio, came into the kitchen, complaining that he was hungry and couldn't he have a meatball? Great-grandma, hearing the boys in the kitchen, came down from her attic bedroom and started fishing meatballs out of the huge pot of sauce on the stove to give to the little boys.

Aunt Maria yelled at Great-grandma for filling the bowl with too many. "One each!" she said. "That's enough for now."

Whatever Aunt Maria's big surprise was got lost in the meat-balls and the stuffed mushrooms and my mother's cake and Grand-ma's chickens, and I just sat there, trying to think up some way to get back on the subject of Aunt Maria's big surprise. Finally, after the boys ate their meatballs and Great-grandma went outside with them to play games, my aunts and my mother sat at the kitchen table, sipping coffee and Anisette.

"Okay, Maria, let's talk about it. Maria has a new idea—come on, tell them."

"Well, I was in Dr. Bernardo's office last week, in the waiting room. There was another woman there. I thought she looked fa-miliar. Then I remembered I used to see her a lot in the A&P. She's older than us, maybe in her fifties, and always looks nice, you know, nice hair and shoes, and always had..."

"Ahem," my mother fake-coughed, nudging Aunt Maria's arm.

"Oh, yeah. Well, I asked her if she lived nearby and she said, "Yes, I've lived in the apartment building on Center Street for the past thirty years."

"Wow," I said, "'Thirty years in the same place. How can you stand it?'"

"Well," she said, "after we'd lived ten years in the same apartment, I started asking my husband about moving. So my husband says to me, 'Listen Doris, we can't afford to move. Maybe we could paint the living room, get new curtains, you know, things like that.' I felt sorry for him. I could see he felt bad that we couldn't afford a move. So I started looking around the apartment to see what I could do to make it look different. The next day, when I was getting dressed in my bedroom, I noticed out the window that there were two nice trees out there—we're on the fourth floor—and a nice view of the church on Locust Avenue, and I thought, "Wow, This could be a nice view for a living room. And that's how it all started."

When I asked her "That's how what started?" she said, "That's when I decided, then and there, that my bedroom would become my living room and my living room would become my bedroom. So we would be moving, but within our own apartment. When I told Leo, he was all for it. I think he was relieved that I'd be happy even though we couldn't move. So he brought some of his friends home from his job and they moved everything all around. It was a madhouse while they were doing it. And I made them change things around in each room a lot of times, but finally, it was done. Then Leo painted the two rooms different colors and it looked like a new apartment. I was so happy. So now we do it every couple of years. My sisters think I'm nuts, but I love it."

"So," she said, "that's how I have stayed in the same apartment for thirty years."

There was a silence.

Then Aunt Maria said, "So, what do you think?"

"Nice story," Aunt Maggie said.

"Yeah, so what are you saying, Maria?" Aunt Angie asked.

"Come on. We know what she's saying," my mother said. "Go ahead, Maria."

"Well, I've been thinking about moving again, and I'm wondering if maybe I should do what Doris did instead."

"Oh Jesus, Mary and Joseph, Maria, that's crazy." Aunt Maggie said.

Aunt Angie added, "Yeah, Maria. What difference would it make? You'd still be in the same house."

"I know," Aunt Maria said, "but it would be a change. And it wouldn't cost anything."

"And it would mean a lot less work for everyone," my mother added. She glared at Aunts Maggie and Angie.

Aunt Maggie said, "Well, I guess that's true."

I thought it was the best idea I ever heard. I couldn't wait to watch them do it and see how it turns out. And I wondered if my brother would switch rooms with me. Aunt Angie added, "Yeah, well, okay. So when would you want to do it?"

Aunt Maria, her eyes fixed on her coffee, answered, "Um… today?" She looked up.

"Today!" They said together.

"Can't it wait? What's your hurry?"

My mother said, "Well, why not get it over with?"

"Oh god!" Aunt Maggie said and let out a loud sigh. "Okay. So when?"

My mother said, "Right after dinner."

"Okay Clara, you can have the pleasure of telling the men what they'll be doing after dinner instead of playing cards," Aunt Maggie said, looking at Aunt Angie as she spoke.

"Yeah, Clara, have fun doing that," Aunt Angie said, chuckling. My mother rolled her eyes.

My mother made the announcement while the men were pouring the wine at the table and the women were setting the foods down for the long Sunday dinner.

First they laughed when my mother—who didn't like to beat

around the bush, but sometimes did—said, "After dinner, you guys have a little job to do at Maria's house."

"What? This can't be true—even Maria can't be moving again, already. We just moved her a few months ago," Uncle Nick said.

"It was a year ago, Nick," my mother corrected. "But this time you are all going to be very surprised about what she's doing."

"Oh goody! I just love surprises. So let's hear this great surprise," Uncle Mike said, folding his arms and leaning back.

My mother said, "Well, this time she's not moving to a different house."

Uncle Vinnie said, "She's finally going to the Looney Bin." He laughed at his own joke.

"Shut up, Vinnie. That's where you belong." Aunt Angie said. Everyone laughed.

I saw a familiar look on my mother's face: annoyed.

"Can we stick to the subject here?" she said, "Maria wants to move some things in her house."

"Oh! Some things—that's nothing. So we'll do it after dinner. What did you want to move, Maria?" Uncle Nick said, sipping his wine.

"Um…uh…" Aunt Maria looked at my mother, who nodded for her to go on. "I want to move my bedroom to where my living room is now and my living room to where my bedroom is?"

Silence. My uncles' faces looked blank.

Then, Uncles Mike, Nick and Vinnie, speaking all at the same time, said, "What?" Uncle Mike said, as if he hadn't heard what he heard.

"What the hell?" Uncle Nick, puzzled.

"What the hell are you talking about?" Uncle Vinnie asked.

"What the hell kind of crackpot idea is that?" my father said, looking at my mother, whom he knew had known about it before but hadn't told him.

Maria, explaining, said, "Well, I met this woman, Doris, at Dr. Bernardo's office the other day, and she told me about..."

"Listen Maria," my mother said, "You don't have to tell the whole story to these big *chadrools*. She wants to switch the living room and the bedroom. That's all there is to it. And you guys will have to do it for her after all she's done for you, all your lives! It's a heck of a lot less work than moving her to a new house, so you're getting off easy. So after dinner, that's what you're all doing. No more discussion—nobody cares about your dumb opinions." My mother sat down. "So let's eat."

For the next few minutes, my uncles looked at each other, complaining and shaking their heads...until my grandfather, tapping his glass with his spoon until all were silent, stood, raised his glass, and in his most commanding voice, said:

"Salute! La Famiglia!" Everyone raised glasses.

"Yeah, yeah, La Famiglia!" the men repeated sarcastically, and sipped their wine. It was settled.

The after-dinner coffee and Sambucca, the ricotta pie and my mother's orange-cream cake, the grapes and cheeses, the nuts and chocolate mints, were all consumed at a very slow pace, while my aunts and my mother rushed through the cleanup and tried to get the men to "quit stalling"—a favorite expression my mother used when my brother and I tried to delay bedtime. Finally, my father got out of his chair.

"Okay. Let's get going. I want to get home before the last ferry, or you'll have to put us all up for the night," he said.

My uncles groaned, got up and walked slowly to the stairs.

"Where's Maria?" Uncle Nick asked.

"She's gone home to get things ready for the move," Aunt Angie explained. "Come on, let's go."

So everybody—Uncles Nick, Mike, Vinnie, Freddie, my father, my aunts Angie, Maggie, my mother, and my older cousin, Nicky, and my brother—all walked next door to my Aunt Maria's and, entering through the back door, yelled, "We're here!"

Uncle Vinnie yelled, "The Patrino Moving Company! At your service!"

"Oh My God! Oh My God! Oh my God!" Aunt Maria shouted from the living room. "You're here!" She ran into the kitchen, her face flushed, her hair all bushy and sticking out, her eyes wide and filled with tears. My mother and Aunts Maggie and Angie moved in close to Aunt Maria and sat her down at the kitchen table. My aunts and I sat around the table with her. My mother brought Aunt Maria a glass of water.

"Yeah! What did you think? Of course we're here. Okay, so, let's see what's what here," Uncle Vinnie started down the hallway to Aunt Maria's bedroom.

Uncle Nick and my father started walking through the dining room to the living room. Uncle Mike went to the back hallway, then to the front hallway into the living room, followed by Uncle Freddie.

"Looks like we'll have to go through the hallway to the bedroom," Uncle Nick said.

"Why? I think we should go right through the dining room and the kitchen into that little hallway to the bedroom," Uncle Freddie said, walking his route as he spoke.

"That's stupid," Uncle Mike said. "Why go that way— through two rooms, when the hallway is more direct?"

"Because it's a narrow hallway and the sofa won't be easy to turn around to get into the bedroom from that angle," my father said.

"Yeah, but where will we put it anyway? There's no room in the bedroom until we get the bed out," Uncle Nick said. "Wait. Let's go look at it," Uncle Mike said. And they all went to the bedroom.

"We should start by taking the bed apart," my father said.

"But where will we put it after we take it apart if we don't get the living room furniture out first?" Uncle Vinnie asked, turning around in a circle. "I mean, Jesus, what a mess we've gotten ourselves into!"

My father, a great fan of Laurel and Hardy movies, said, "Take it easy, Ollie. We'll figure it out."

"Yeah, we'll figure it out," Uncle Mike said. Then, turning to my father and lowering his voice, he said, "How do we figure it out, Jimmy?"

"Well," my father said, speaking very fast, "Suppose we take the bed apart, move the dining room furniture to one side of the room and put the bed pieces in there, then we can take the sofa and bring it to the bedroom where the bed was, then we can take the bed pieces from the dining room and put the bed back together in the living room—and we can do the same with the rest of the pieces. As we move pieces out of the bedroom, we can put them in the dining room, move the living room furniture into the bedroom and then move the bedroom furniture we have in the dining room into the living room—and we can keep doing that until we're done. Yeah. That'll work."

"Huh?" Uncle Vinnie said.

"What?" Uncle Mike said.

My cousin Nick and my brother were laughing hysterically.

"Uhmm…uh…yeah. I think it'll work," Uncle Nick said, scratching his head.

Uncle Freddie, laughing, said, "Well, I don't know what the hell you just said, Jimmy, but you're the only one who seems to know how to do it, so I'm in."

And so they began, following my father's plan, while we stayed in the kitchen, made coffee, had some cookies that Aunt Maria baked as the men did the move, and did our part, which my father explained was to "stay out of the way until further notice."

We stayed out of the way, but we could hear the men arguing

about where things should go and my father telling them again and again: "First bring the bedroom furniture to the dining room, then move…"

"No," Uncle Nick said to Uncle Mike, "Don't put that back in the old bedroom—it goes in the old living room."

"Oh, Jesus," my father yelled, "You're putting the bedroom furniture in the living room before removing the living room furniture—there's just this beg mess of furniture in one room and nothing in the other!" My father was shouting now.

"So where should I put this?" Uncle Mike asked, holding up a side table from the living room.

"In the dining room," Uncle Freddie said.

"This is the stupidest thing I've ever done," Uncle Mike said.

"No, it's not, Mike," Uncle Freddie explained. "It only gets stupid when you think about it."

"Don't think!" my father shouted.

During all of this, my brother and Cousin Nick are sometimes laughing out loud, sometimes stifling it, as they move some of the smaller furniture pieces.

"Those kids are the only ones getting it right," my father says.

"Yeah, well nothing sounds stupid to kids," Uncle Mike says.

"Hey, wait a minute. I just moved that out of the old bedroom to the new bedroom and now I find it back in the old bedroom. What the hell?" Uncle Nick said, his voice rising as he spoke.

"Well, isn't that a living room piece?" Uncle Freddie asked.

"No, it's a bedside table," Uncle Nick answered.

"Holy shit!" my father said. "What is this, a Marx Brother's movie?" My father often sees life as a scene in a comic movie. "Okay," he says. "There are just too many of us. That's the problem. You, Groucho, Harpo and Chico, you stay, and Larry, Curly and Mo, maybe you should go."

There was a momentary pause.

"Yeah, well I volunteer to leave," Uncle Vinnie said. "I can think of lots of things I'd rather do."

"Well, you can stop for now, but you have to stick around to help move that heavy double dresser and lift the mattress and box spring," my father said.

"So there's nobody else who can do that?" Uncle Vinnie said, looking around at the men, who had all stopped working and were gathered in the dining room. As he looked at each one, they shook their heads 'no.'

"Just you and Mike," my father said.

"Okay, I'll go have coffee with the women," Uncle Vinnie said.

"Yeah, and take Mike with you," my father said.

"I don't want any coffee," Uncle Mike said. "Let's get this done. C'mon." He grabbed the vanity chair.

"I volunteer to go to the kitchen," Uncle Freddie said.

"Yeah. Go," my father said, dropping into a living room chair in the dining room, holding his head in his hands.

Somehow, after about another hour, everything was in the room it was supposed to be in. Aunt Maria then had the uncles move the furniture around in each room until things were situated as she had envisioned.

Further notice came when my father appeared in the kitchen.

"Okay, time for the women's touches," my father announced. It was time to move small lamps and remake the bed, hang the switched curtains, and set things on the tables and vanity in just the way Aunt Maria wanted. When we were finished, we all took the tour of the new layout. It felt strange, but it certainly looked like a different place, and Aunt Maria was as happy as I had seen her the day she first moved into that house.

"Mission Accomplished!" my father toasted, as the men crowded into the kitchen for a glass of wine.

"As Papa would say," Uncle Nick said, *"Salute! La Famiglia!"*

Felicitazioni

AT THE END OF THAT SUMMER, I turned twelve and started Junior
High School. In Beacon, the junior high was located in the older
part of the high school building. During the first few months of the
new school year, I wasn't much interested in what was happening
in my mother's family in Newburgh. I was fully involved with my
exciting new environment, where high school students looked like
adults, and they used the same gym and auditorium, walked many
of the same halls we twelve-year-olds walked. We now changed
classrooms after each class and the students from the other elementa-
ry school were all added to our classes, so there were lots of new kids
to meet, lots of chaotic moments as we got used to so much that was
new. Such fun.

It wasn't until the second Sunday in November that I became
aware of Uncle Danny's quieter, thinner appearance, and while he
did smile at me and ask me how school was going as he walked by,
he wouldn't speak when my aunts or my mother tried to get him
into a conversation. Just a quick one-word answer then he turned
away, as if in a hurry to get somewhere.

At that Sunday dinner, the week before Thanksgiving, Uncle
Vinnie announced that he and Josephine were to be married two
weeks before Christmas, on December 10.

"It won't be a big wedding," he explained. "It's going to be very simple. Josephine and her mother are planning everything. There will be no bridesmaids, just two ushers, no big fancy reception, just a ceremony in Josephine's church, then a dinner for the two families in her uncle's restaurant. Danny will be my best man and her cousin Marion will be the maid-of honor."

I looked at everyone at the table after Uncle Vinnie's announcement and noted that my aunts and uncles all smiled at Uncle Vinnie and Josephine. They all said, "Congratulations," but though they said the right words, the good wishes sounded very quiet and polite. Uncle Vinnie did generate some excitement when he announced that the restaurant Josephine's Uncle Sal owned was Carmelle's—a very expensive, fancy Italian restaurant on the river that everyone knew of, but hardly anyone had ever been to. Everyone seemed surprised that someone as plain as Josephine would have an uncle who owned such a fancy place. After this news about Carmelle's, Grandpa tapped his wine glass with his spoon, and when everyone rose and held up their glasses, he offered, "Salute! Felicitazioni!"

Everyone joined in, a "Felicitazioni!" with a bit more enthusiasm.

I noticed that Uncle Danny put an arm around Uncle Vinnie as he shook his hand. Then he hugged Josephine. Although he was smiling, his eyes looked watery, and he walked away and up the stairs, quietly, slowly. In a few minutes, we could hear him on the parlor piano, playing a song I remembered Grandpa singing at one of the musicales held on Grandpa's front porch during the summer. Grandpa had sung it in Italian, so I didn't know what the words were saying, but the sound of it had made my eyes fill with tears. Now, hearing Uncle Danny play it, I heard the heartbreak even more. Was he sad that his brother would be leaving the house they had grown up in, leaving him as the last bachelor? Or did he miss Phillie and wish that he could be announcing his marriage, to her? Whatever it was that, I knew his heart hurt, and mine hurt with him.

The next week was Thanksgiving. My grandmother, my mother, and all my aunts participated in preparing the Thanksgiving Feast. My grandmother was in charge, and each aunt cooked her specialty. My mother was the champion lasagna maker, so she owned that course. My Aunt Maggie, who, though she was not Italian, was, to everyone's amazement, a pretty decent cook. She prepared the sweet potato casserole. My Aunt Angie prepared the Antipasto—she was artistic and made the huge platters of specially-prepared meats and cheeses and vegetables into works of art. Grandma roasted two turkeys, each with a different stuffing, one chestnut and one sausage. The others made the mashed potatoes, the string beans and almonds, the peas and mushrooms, the creamed onions, the stuffed artichokes, the fresh cranberry sauce, the gravy, the rolls—and each baked their favorite pie. There were twenty-five for dinner, and enough food for fifty.

At the kids table, we stood and watched as if seeing a spectacle, a circus. Grandpa, at the head of the table, carved one of the turkeys; Uncle Nick at the table's other end, carved the other. All my aunts bustled up and down the cellar steps, carting one delectable dish after another. As they arrived at the table with a dish, they announced it so all could hear: "The sweet potato casserole!" "The peas and mushrooms!" "The Sausage Stuffing!" "The Stringbeans and Almonds!" "The glazed carrots!" "THE GRAVY!" "The Cranberries!" "The Rolls!" "The Chestnut Stuffing!" "The Mashed Potatoes!"

On and on, until everything was on the table. As each dish arrived at the table, my uncles would exclaim and applaud. Each was served in two serving bowls or platters, one at each end of the long table. Kids had to go to parents, who made up a dinner plate for each of us to take back to the kids' table. When everyone at both tables was served, Grandpa signaled the toast and all stood, raised glasses for the blessing: "Thank you God, for this wonderful food, for our good appetites, for our family, and most of all, thank God for these angels, who prepared this feast with great skill and great love. We thank you, God, and we thank these beautiful women for this glorious feast."

Grandpa put his glass down and began to applaud. All my uncles and all my cousins joined in, applauding and whistling and calling out, "Brava! Brava!" My grandmother, my aunts and my mother smiled, nodded to each other, and curtsied.

"God bless all of us here today, and bless the one who is far away, but here in our hearts. Salute! La Famiglia!"

"Oh! He mentioned Bella!" my mother whispered to Aunt Maria.

"I think he's forgiven her." Aunt Maria said, her eyes filled with tears.

"I don't know about that, Maria. But he still loves her."

The feast lasted all day. At our table we had a wonderful time with Anginonna, who stole lots of chocolates from the adult table and put walnuts on the seats of anyone who got up, so that they would squeal when they came back and sat down. Whenever she saw an opportunity, she would switch dessert plates on people and then wait for them to try to find their own. Anginonna knew all sorts of ways to trick and frustrate the adults. We joined in and had such fun outsmarting them. But it was a Holiday and everyone forgave us and laughed when they figured it out.

On the ferry that night, on our way home, I thought about Uncle Vinnie getting married two weeks before Christmas. I remembered something Uncle Danny had said to my mother the day she tried to talk to him. My mother had told him that when Uncle Vinnie got married, he'd be the last bachelor in the family. He'd made a joke about his gravestone: Here lies Danny Hot Dog, the last bachelor. I remembered she told Aunt Maria it "gave her the creeps."

When Uncle Vinnie made his announcement at the dinner table, his bride-to-be, Josephine, sat silently at his side in her light grey sweater-set and long string of pearls, which she kept twisting and untwisting. She was "always fidgeting," Aunt Maria said, "always fidgeting with something." I had never heard the word fidgeting, but I knew what it meant when Aunt Maria said it because Josephine did it every time I saw her. And it was the perfect word to describe it. Poor Josephine. Everyone found fault with her. We couldn't help ourselves. We all wanted Uncle Vinnie to marry his old girlfriend that we all loved, Penny. We had lost Penny, and now we seem to have lost Phillie, too.

Lost in my own thoughts, I missed the conversation my parents, in the front seat, were having. I caught the last thing my mother said: "Well. We're going to have to accept her. She'll be a member of the family, whether we like it or not. We'll have to find something about her to like. After all, none of this is her fault."

"Well," my father added, "I already like her better than your big-shot brother. He's the *cretino* who dumped the one he should be marrying. Josephine's just the innocent replacement."

Yes, I thought, the innocent replacement. Poor Josephine, the woman nobody likes. And poor Uncle Danny, the one man left, the last bachelor. What would become of him?

The Last Bachelor

I GUESS THIS IS HOW IT HAPPENS: except for old or very sick people, we don't expect death.

There's no graceful, appropriate, right time for it. It's always a shock that no one is ever prepared for. And in my large, loud, talkative, Italian family, with so much always happening? Death just doesn't fit in. There's no place to put it.

And there's no way to understand how, when we're having our second helping of lasagne, the men arguing about who made the best wine and what's the best route to the Yonkers Raceway, the women complaining about their hairdresser and the children and the price of pork chops, how do we make a place for death?

And how, when we all believe we know each other, understand each other, help each other, love each other, how then could one of us fall into some empty, horrible crack, and slip away so far, so alone?

Gone. Just gone.

Grandma had gone up the stairs to tell him to come down, that Maria had made his favorite, ricotta pie. "I'll go get Danny," she said in a bustle, and then from the attic room over the parlor at the front of the house, a scream so terrible—a scream to freeze the spine—a scream, heard over and over again when we tried to sleep, for months and months—and just when we think it's over because we didn't hear it for a night or two, suddenly there it was again.

The screams—not one scream. One and then another and then another—and another, as if there was nothing else to do, to say, but scream—nothing in the world as right as a scream—and "No! No! No!" Then my mother and Aunts Maria and Angie running to the screams—my father and uncles Mike and Nick running after them. My Grandfather standing frozen.

"I don't want to know. I don't want to know," he whispered again and again, "I don't want to know."

"You kids stay here. Don't follow us," my father said as he ran to the stairs.

But we could hear it all: the screams, then, *"Morte! Morte! Morte!"* my grandmother, screaming, sobbing, "Danny—my baby—Danny. Why? Why? Why? And all the others, my parents, my aunts, my uncles, crying out, "No! No! No, Danny! No!"

And my grandfather, standing still in the middle of the kitchen.

Aunt Angie came down the stairs, looked at Grandpa, went to him, put her arms around him. "Come on, Papa. Come with me to your room. You need to lie down. I'm going to get Mama. You both have to rest. We can take care of everything."

Grandpa pushed her away, went to the stairs, Aunt Angie ran after, tried to hold him back.

"No, Papa, don't go up there. Don't, Papa." She followed him up the stairs.

Uncle Freddie came down.

"You kids get your coats. You're coming with me to my house. Your parents want you out of here. I'll stay with you over there. It will be alright—we'll have some hot chocolate. I'll turn on the TV if you want."

I heard my Grandpa yelling, "No! No! No! Danny, No!" and then sobbing, mixed with moans that filled the house as we put our coats on and ran out the back door, across the street, to Uncle Freddie's, to the quiet rooms that always smelled like bleach, and the fresh bread Aunt Angie baked every morning.

I was shivering. Uncle Freddie asked me if I was cold. I said I didn't know, but he took a small blanket from the sofa and wrapped it around my shoulders.

"It's alright," he said, "you'll be alright. Just sit down here and I'll bring you some hot cocoa. It will stop the shivering."

I sat on the sofa, where I could see Grandpa's house across the narrow street. It was all going on there —the screaming, the sobbing, the moaning, the crying out. And Uncle Danny—dead. My Uncle Danny. What happened to him? Why did he die? My brother came and sat next to me. My cousins sat on the carpet at our feet. We didn't speak. Some of them were crying quietly. My brother put his arm around my shoulders. He had tears in his eyes, but he wasn't crying out loud. Uncle Freddie brought a tray carrying cups of hot cocoa for all of us and went back for a tray of Aunt Angie's biscotti. We drank the cocoa, but I couldn't eat the biscotti. We stayed there a long time, not talking. Then my parents came in. My mother looked pale and worn out. Her eyes were swollen and red. My father asked Uncle Freddie for some cocoa for my mother. She came to the sofa. My brother and I moved apart to let her sit between us. She put an arm around each of us.

"You alright?" she asked.

"What happened to him?" I asked her. "What happened to Uncle Danny?"

"We don't know for sure. We think he took too many pills. He had pills from the doctor for how nervous he always got. But we think he took too many. A terrible mistake. Poor Danny. A terrible mistake."

"But maybe he...do you...do you think maybe he did it on purpose?" my brother asked, tears filling his eyes, brimming over.

My eyes filled with tears, too.

"Oh Mom, did he, Did he do it on purpose?" I could barely speak.

My mother, wiping her tears with her flowered handkerchief, said, "No. We don't believe he did it on purpose."

My father came back with cocoa for my mother, "Don't ask your mother so many questions right now. She's very upset. We all are."

He handed her the cup of cocoa. She took it in both hands, took a sip, then held it close to her chest and closed her eyes for a moment. Then she looked up and out the window towards Grandpa's house.

"No, the kids can ask," she said. "They're upset, too. Oh God, look at them. Freddie, can the kids stay here tonight? Maria and Angie and I want to stay with Mama and Papa tonight. Or maybe Jimmy and the kids can stay at Maria's. I don't know. I can't think straight."

Uncle Freddie told her not to worry, that he would figure it all out and she should just do what she needed to do. My brother stayed at Uncle Freddie's with my cousins Dickey, Freddie and Duke. All my older girl cousins went together to Uncle Nick's. I stayed at Aunt Maria's with my father and Uncle John. Uncle John made a big bowl of pastina, which was the perfect thing to eat that night. I thought I'd never be able to sleep in Aunt Maria's guest room, but I fell asleep as soon as I got in bed and pulled up the silky blue quilt that smelled like Aunt Maria's perfume.

When morning came, I opened my eyes in the guest room, so full of Aunt Maria: her old photos of family who had come from Italy when they were young, in carved wooden frames. A round little rosewood table and two matching chairs that fit perfectly in the bay window, blush-tinted sheer curtains, bowls of rose petals on the marble-top bedside tables, her famous hats on the wicker hat stand, and the wallpaper—tiny red roses and pale green vines on a light pink background on every wall. The carpet was the blue of the sky on a perfect day. I looked at each part of the room, feeling I had entered a fairy tale and I was the Princess in her royal bedroom.

Then a sound in the hallway, voices from the kitchen, and the smell of coffee brewing, reminded me...no, it was no fairy tale. It was sad and scary, and horrible. My Uncle Danny was dead. I would never see him again, never hear his voice, never hear him play his beautiful songs on the piano. There must be something I should do. But what? What could any of us do but cry, and ask, "Why?"

The next few days everyone came to Grandpa and Grandma's house: aunts and uncles and cousins, kids, customers and barbers from Grandpa's barbershop and Uncle Danny's musician friends. Uncle Danny's body had been taken away and brought back to lie in a coffin in the parlor, right next to the piano he loved to play. The whole house was filled with flowers sent by family and friends, and although the fragrance was sweet, it filled the air with sadness. Uncle Danny would have loved them. He had always tended the gardens and the pots of flowers Grandma put on the porch for the summer.

We kids were told we could go in to see Uncle Danny and say goodbye or not, that it was our choice. I wanted to see him, my favorite Uncle, to say goodbye and tell him I loved him and would always miss him. But when I got close to the coffin and saw his face, I felt so scared, I could only cry and back away to where my brother and my cousins were in the dining room, near the kitchen.

"I told you not to do it," my brother said. But he put his arm around the back of my chair and patted my shoulder.

"It didn't look like him," I said.

"People don't look the same after they're dead," he said.

I wondered how he knew that, but I didn't ask. He always knew stuff. I was just glad he was there because I was shaking again, and I was so scared. I didn't know why. I always wanted to be with my brother when I was scared. Once, during a very bad lightning storm, I had been screaming and crying because I was so scared. After it was over, I told him that I knew I acted like a baby, but he said, "No you don't. Sometimes we're supposed to be scared. When there's really something to be scared of, we're supposed to be scared, so we'll look for a way to be safe." When I got a little older, I realized how nice he was to make me feel better when I was so embarrassed. Not many people are that nice. My brother—and my Uncle Danny.

On the third day of the wake, my mother told us that it was the day of the funeral. It was to be at St. Mary's Church, which was the parish where Uncle Danny had gone to school when he was a child. It was a drizzly day, very dark and foggy, the kind of day everyone hated. Everyone but me. I loved this kind of rainy day, loved watching the rain from my bedroom window, making everything clean and new.

Not today. Today the rain fell like tears, soaking the world in sadness.

My mother came to where all the cousins, including my brother and me, were sitting in the dining room, out of view of Uncle Danny's body in the coffin. She explained that Father Donorfrio would come to say prayers, then the funeral parlor would be sending a hearse to pick up Uncle Danny's body. Then the coffin would be closed and taken to the church for Mass and then to the cemetery to be buried. So, she said, if any of us wanted to say goodbye to Uncle Danny, this would be our last chance. She said she would stand with any of us who didn't want to stand there alone. I looked at my cousins. They all looked so scared. In that moment, I realized what I was scared of —I was scared of my dead Uncle Danny—scared of looking right into his dead face, knowing he would never again open his eyes, speak a word, move a hand. He was gone. I didn't want to see his dead body. I wanted to remember him playing the piano, laughing with his girlfriend, Phillie.

And I didn't want to look at…*morte.*

My older cousin, Catherine, knelt at the coffin to pray, my mother standing close to her. It had been very quiet until then. But

there was a sudden ruckus in the kitchen. We couldn't see what it
was, but there was shouting and crying and scrambling and calling
out: "Clara! Maria! Mama! Papa! Oh my god! You came! Aunt
Angie came to the doorway and cried out: "Bella is here! Bella is
really here!

My mother, Grandma, Grandpa, and my uncles and aunts, who
had been in the parlor about to pray with Father Donorfrio, hurried to the kitchen, where Bella was standing, sobbing. The whole
family surrounded her, hugging her, crying, answering her questions
about Uncle Danny's death. We kids stayed in the doorway, silently
watching. I could hardly believe my eyes. My Aunt Bella had come
back. Grandpa stood next to me in the doorway, silently watching.
His eyes, filled with tears, were fixed on Aunt Bella, but he stood
perfectly still.

Slowly emerging from the caresses and the crying and the talk
of Uncle Danny's death, Aunt Bella turned her head and seeing
Grandpa, whispered, "Papa! Oh, Papa."

They stood silently looking at each other for a moment. Then
Grandpa opened his arms to her and she ran into them. He buried
his head into her bright red hair and sobbed, "Bella, Bella. My
little Bella!"

Everyone watched, my aunts and my mother smiling and
crying at the same time. No one had been sure if Grandpa would
have welcomed her or not. I thought their tears must have been the
"happy tears" my mother had told me about. This was the first time
I understood what that meant.

At the church, we kids were instructed to enter first. The first
few rows had black satin bows at the ends, where we couldn't sit.
My brother and I sat with our cousins, all together in two rows.

An organ began to play, and the children's choir began to sing.
I knew the song from my own choir: "Holy God, we praise thy
name." As the singing began, the procession started. First was the

coffin. Carrying it were my father, my Uncles Freddie, John, my oldest cousin, Nick, and two of Uncle Danny's friends. Just behind it were Grandpa and Grandma, with my uncles Vinnie, Mike and Nick, walking slowly, their arms linked. After them were my mother and her sisters, Aunts Maria, Angie, and Bella. They held hands as they walked to their pew and sat together through the Mass, seated just behind Grandpa and Grandma in the first two rows.

There was no talking, no crying, just the sound of the singing and then the priest beginning the Mass. At the end of the Mass, when the pall bearers were carrying the casket out with the family following, it seemed everyone was crying. Though Uncle Danny had died, he had still been with us.

But the time spent with Uncle Danny's body was soon to be over, and now he would be buried and everyone would leave him there, in the ground. I couldn't find a way to think about that without feeling sad and horrified about what would happen to him.

After the Mass and the Burial, everyone gathered at Aunt Maria's. A crowd of about forty people arrived, many of them bringing foods they had prepared: several spaghetti pies, trays of breads and cheeses, olives and *caponata,* platters of roasted vegetables, bowls of meatballs in sauce, baking pans of eggplant parmigiana, sausage and peppers, and assorted cookies, cakes and pies, and wine, soda, coffee. People just seemed to know what to do, what to bring, how to feed the people who had come from a short or a long distance to be with us, to help us through this horribly sad time. There was lots of talking, then Uncle Vinnie and some of Uncle Danny's musician friends announced that they would play a few of Uncle Danny's favorite tunes. Some of them were songs Uncle Danny often played alone, in the parlor. Hearing them played now made some of us cry a little, but there was something good about hearing them this one last time. Soon after the music, the people began to leave, until only my aunts and uncles and cousins remained. Aunt Bella was sitting with my mother and my aunts, including my Aunts Connie and Maggie—and Josephine, who would soon become my aunt, too. Now that Uncle Danny was gone, Uncle Vinnie had to choose another best man. He chose their cousin, Rocco, who was to marry the girl he found in Italy who looked just like me. I was glad I would have another chance to see her at Uncle Vinnie's wedding.

After a while, talking about Uncle Vinnie's wedding, Aunt Maria asked Aunt Bella where she would be staying.

"Oh, at Tom's, with Toomie," she said.

"Oh," Aunt Maria said, "And Tom is okay with you being there?"

"Well, he's staying at his sister's while I'm here," Aunt Bella said.

"Then where will you stay?" Aunt Angie asked.

"I'll be leaving to go back home," Aunt Bella said, a note of regret in her voice.

"You mean you aren't staying?" my mother sounded surprised.

"No, Clara. I just came because of Danny. I couldn't not be here for my brother's funeral. But I can't stay."

"Oh my God," Aunt Maria said, her eyes filling with tears. "I thought you would stay, Bella. Don't you want to be here with Toomie?"

"I've been talking to Tom and we're working out a way for Toomie to stay with me during the summer. And we're going to meet half-way, for short visits. Tom is cooperating. I'll be seeing Toomie, but I'm not coming back here."

"But why can't you and Denzel move back here?" Aunt Angie asked.

"Denzel is a miner, that's all he knows. And we need to have security."

"He could learn another way to earn a living, couldn't he?" Aunt Connie asked.

"Look, we don't have time for that. I'm pregnant." Aunt Bella said, looking up, away from the shock on the faces of her sisters.

"Oh, God, Bella. That's it then. You're stuck with him," Aunt Maria said.

"I'm not stuck. I'm where I want to be, Maria."

"Well can you at least come for visits. We all miss you. Papa misses you, and now he's going to be having a hard time without Danny. Can you do that?" my mother asked.

"I guess so, but we don't have extra money for traveling."

"We'll chip in for that, Bella. Won't we?" She turned to the rest of them.

"Yes, we will "Aunt Angie said. "You don't have to worry about that."

"Then I'll come," Aunt Bella said. She was crying.

"We'll make sure we get to see you," my mother said, reaching out and grabbing her hand,

"Don't worry, Bella, we'll come to see you, too. Would that be alright? I mean, would Denzel be okay with us coming?"

"Oh yes. Denzel would like that," Aunt Bella said.

"Then it's settled. We'll just travel back and forth. That's all there is to it," Aunt Angie said. "It's not the end of the world."

"So when's this baby due?" Aunt Maria asked.

"June," Aunt Bella said. "The middle of June." She wiped her tears with a paper napkin Aunt Maria handed her.

"Well, we'll make sure we get there for that," my mother said, putting her hand over Aunt Bella's. "Don't you worry, you'll have your sisters for that."

After Uncle Danny was buried, I had dreams of him every night. Sometimes I would see him at the piano, playing the beautiful sad music that I now know were sometimes Chopin Nocturnes, sometimes standard ballads. Sometimes I would see him with Phillie, laughing at Sunday dinner, pouring her glasses of wine, smiling and talking. Sometimes I would see him as he looked in the casket, his face blank, his skin a strange gray color, wearing a dark jacket and white shirt and a silky, pale-blue tie, the color of his eyes. In my dreams, his eyes were so full of light and so pale, a color more white than blue—and I could see through them to the blue heaven where I was sure he had gone. Then I would awaken and remember that I would never see those blue eyes again. Other times I would see him in the casket, underground, with all the things I'd ever heard about being dead: hair and fingernails that keep growing, worms eating the flesh, body slowly turning to dust, all happening to poor Uncle Danny, who had never hurt a single soul his whole life, who had never had any woman really love him, who was always kind to all the kids in the family, who walked away from the men's arguments and smiled at great-Grandma's antics. He had wandered alone through his quiet life.

Uncle Danny—the kindest, most gentle man I ever knew. I would wake up crying and angry. Why is he underground in that wooden box while the rest of us are up here? Why do some people die long before they are old? And though my mother told me, no, I still wondered if Uncle Danny really did take too many pills on purpose, because he had become just too sad to be alive? Sometimes I would say things to Uncle Danny, knowing he couldn't hear me, but some small part of me believed that maybe he could. I would tell him I loved him and would always remember him and that he had made the world more beautiful with his wonderful music.

A week after the funeral, Aunt Bella had to leave. My mother and my Aunts Maria, Angie, Connie and Maggie stood on Aunt Maria's porch, crying and shivering in the cold December morning. I watched from the doorway while they each gave her a teary hug. Just before she went down the five steps to the street, she blew me a kiss and waved to me, which made me cry.

"Oh no!" she shouted from the street, "Don't cry, I'll be back."

The Wedding

WHEN THE FAMILY FINALLY TURNED THEIR ATTENTION to Uncle Vinnie's wedding, they found their part in the plans for it amounted to sending out reminders of the day, the time, and the place. All the preparations had been taken care of by Josephine and her family. The night before the wedding, Uncle Vinnie held a Rehearsal Dinner, at the nightclub where he played piano on Saturday nights. It was an odd night, with music played by a small band of Uncle Vinnie's friends, and foods unfamiliar and delicious to most of us, but inedible to my father, who believed only Italian food was safe and worthy of being eaten. He asked the waiter to get him a cheese sandwich and made a face when it was served to him on sliced American bread, which he peeked under, lifting the top slice with two fingers and dropping it back immediately, exclaiming, "Mayonnaise! Jesus, Clara—" he seemed to think my mother was to blame) "—it's got goddam mayonnaise on it!" Mayonnaise was poison, according to him, and the look of horror on his face convinced me that he truly believed that. Josephine's family looked stunned. Our family, used to my father's distrust of non-Italian foods and people, hardly noticed.

The wedding the next day was quiet and orderly, like an assembly at school. People formed lines and filled pews as instructed by the ushers. I was surprised at how many people were there. Uncle Vinnie had said it was to be just family, and I guess it was, but both families were pretty large. I counted all the people in church—there were sixty-six people! The priest read the mass in Latin, the vows were recited in Italian and repeated in English. The bride, carrying a bouquet of pink roses, and wearing an ankle-length white satin dress and a small matching hat with a veil that fell down over her eyes, actually looked kind of pretty. She smiled all day long, sitting at a special table with Uncle Vinnie, who drank steadily all day long, filling his glass from the bottles of wine at his table. A very tall and ornate wedding cake had been placed on a small table before them. I wondered if the many flowers that decorated each layer were edible.

The dinner was extraordinary. It began with cold lobster, shrimp and scallops in a lemony sauce, followed by the main course of osso bucco, which I had never tasted, and risotto and roasted vegetables of many colors, and romaine lettuce with black olives, bits of goat cheese and roasted red peppers. The wedding cake seemed way too beautiful to eat but was delicious, with rum-flavored custard between the layers, whipped cream frosting, and tiny powdered strawberries served with each slice—and the flowers were edible. Everyone there raved about the food, including even my father, who always ordered that cheese sandwich. (My mother had told him on the way in the car that day that if he ordered a cheese sandwich, she was divorcing him. He laughed at that and said, "What if I order a baloney sandwich?" She hit him with her pocketbook.)

After the dinner, the band played what they called, "dance music" and some people danced on the small dance floor. They played standard tunes, interspersed with Italian songs, which many people in both families knew and sang together, for the first time really connecting with each other, singing and dancing Italian dances. When they danced the Tarantella, my Uncle Mike grabbed my hand and pulled me into the circle to dance with them. It was so much fun to be part of the dance, twirling around with my aunts and uncles and Josephine's family. Because I had heard many of the songs on Grandpa's porch in the summer, I was able to sing along with some of them. It was during one of the dances that Lianna, cousin Rocco's wife,—the one I had met at Easter dinner, astonished at how much she looked like me—suddenly appeared at my table, sitting next to me in my mother's vacated chair.

"Ciao!" she said, smiling. I noticed she didn't have the same space between her front teeth that I had.

"Hello." What I could say to this person who looked so much like me that she had to be my sister, or my mother? How else could we look so much alike?

We stared at each other. Then laughed.

"I am learning English," she said.

"Oh, that's good. Are you taking classes?" I asked.

"No. But Rocco's friend's wife is teacher and she teaches me in her house."

"Oh. Well, that's good. Are you working here in Newburgh?"

"Yes. I am *estetista*…uh…" seeing that I didn't understand, she seemed to search for a different word.

"Capello?" She put her hand up to her hair, as if to arrange it differently.

"Hair? Oh! Are you still a hairdresser?"

"Yes! In Mary Spinelli Shop."

"Oh yes. My Aunt Rosie goes there."

"You come. I will cut for you," she said, cocking her head, as if to think of how she would cut it.

"Okay. I'll ask my mother."

Cousin Rocco appeared, stood behind Lianna's chair.

"So how is Lianna's twin? You see how you will look in fifteen years? You'll be as beautiful as Lianna."

"Oh, I hope so," I said, a little embarrassed. I wasn't sure why.

When the band started playing *Funiculi, Funicula,* Lianna began singing with the others, and remembering that song in Italian from last summer, I sang along. She smiled at me and put her arm around my shoulder as we sang together.

On the way home I asked my mother if she had enjoyed the wedding.

"Well, yes, as much as I could without Danny there. We all tried to be happy for Vinnie. He talked about postponing it, but we all thought he should go through with it. Dan would want him to. And we all needed something to be happy about."

"But nobody was very happy that Uncle Vinnie was marrying Josephine instead of Penny," I said, feeling confused.

"Yes, I know, but we're all trying to accept her and his decision. Now that they're married, she's part of the family. I know it's hard to understand but that's what we do. We try to accept the decisions people in the family make, even when we don't agree."

"Oh, like with Aunt Bella?"

"Yes, like with Aunt Bella. We love her, so we accept her decision, though none of us like it."

I didn't fully understand about accepting something they all thought was a mistake, but something about it made me feel better about my family. More safe, somehow.

Christmas

ON SUNDAY MORNING, THE DAY AFTER THE WEDDING, I woke up
to the familiar smell of Sunday sauce simmering on the stove. My
brother was sampling a meatball smothered in it as I stood at the
kitchen doorway dressed for Mass. He said I had too much perfume
on and that the best perfume was the smell of our mother's Sunday
sauce cooking on the stove—so why didn't I dab that behind my ears?

"All the boys will follow you, all over town," he said, "No boy
wants to smell flowers. Boys are hungry. We want to smell food."

I told him he was insane, but I did suspect that he was on to
something. I wasn't that happy with the smell of the Tweed Cologne
that my cousin had sent me for my birthday, which I was allowed to
wear on weekends. And the sauce smelled pretty great. My mother
settled the matter when she turned from the stove and said, "Well,
it's not a bad idea, but it's too soon. When you turn thirty and
you're still single, I think then you should try the sauce behind the
ears. And maybe carry a few meatballs in your purse."

My brother, howling with laughter, left the kitchen for his
room, while my mother, stirring the sauce, told me to eat something
before Mass.

"Mom, don't you realize that Christmas is coming, in exactly
fourteen days? I don't understand why nobody's talking about it."

"Oh yes. I know. We're going to have to get everything done

very fast—just this week and next to do it all. Daddy is getting the tree tomorrow, and I'll be shopping just about every day. But don't worry, we'll get it all done. Don't you want a meatball?"

"No, I'm just having toast," I said, distracted by worry that Christmas wouldn't happen the way it should. With Uncle Danny dead and Aunt Bella gone back to West Virginia, I didn't see how it could be anything like our usual happy Christmas.

"Will we be going to Grandpa's, like we always do?"

"Of course. Why wouldn't we? We always go there. And this year we especially have to be with Grandma and Grandpa after all they've been through.

"Oh…well I thought maybe everyone might not want to have Christmas the way we always used to, now that…"

"No, now don't do that. Uncle Danny is gone and Aunt Bella is somewhere else, but the rest of us are still having Christmas together, and we will still have a nice time at Grandpa's and Grandma's. Even though we'll miss Uncle Danny and Aunt Bella and have sad feelings. But you and the other kids will have the same happy Christmas you all deserve, honey. And I'm sure Uncle Danny and Aunt Bella would want that for all of us. Come here, you little worry wart."

She pulled me to her and hugged me. "We'll all be okay, Honey. You'll see. We'll rush around like crazy the next two weeks and we'll get everything done. You'll help me, won't you? We'll all have to pitch in, that's all."

Feeling better now that I knew my mother had a plan, I decided to have the meatball after all.

The next few days were full of Christmas preparations. My mother spent every day shopping, every night wrapping presents, sometimes hiding things in the attic after kids were assumed to be asleep. My brother and I knew the presents were there, but after getting caught peeking once, the week before Christmas, we stopped our annual hunting-the-presents activities and vowed to each other that we'd never do it again. So, except for the time my mother hid the Flexible Flyer sled for my brother in the back of the bathroom storage closet, I never peeked (and I never told him about the sled.)

We all pitched in to wrap the presents for my aunts and uncles and my cousins. And my brother and I secretly wrapped our presents for our parents, the ones we picked out at the Five and Ten after school, using my allowance money and my brother's paperboy money.

The week before Christmas my mother started baking cookies and talking on the phone to my aunts, about what everyone would cook for the Christmas dinner and who would host the Feast of the Seven Fishes on Christmas Eve. It was decided that Aunt Angie would do Christmas Eve and my mother would help her by cooking the *Zuppa di Pesce* (fish soup) and other fish dishes she was known for. All of these foods had to be cooked just before eating them, so we all had to get to Aunt Angie's early on Christmas Eve. It was fun at her house because she had a very big basement with a ping-pong table and lots of games—and a television set. All the cousins would spend the whole time there, without adults, except for an occasional check-in from an aunt or uncle. Even the men helped with the food preparation, shelling and cleaning the fish and chopping vegetables. It was fun to watch them cooking and drinking wine and singing.

When we could smell the stuffed calamari cooking in the tomato sauce, we knew the feast was almost ready. Although I wouldn't eat the stuffed calamari, I loved the pasta and sauce that came with it. Everyone else loved this dish, my Aunt Maria's specialty, and everyone gathered around Aunt Angie's huge round kitchen table, where all seven fish dishes were served, filling bowls and plates with these once-a-year favorites, carrying them to the dining room to eat and visit and sing Christmas songs in Italian and English, while my mother and my aunts continued cooking, an-

nouncing each dish as it was ready. Everyone cheered the stuffed calamari and the clams posillipo especially, and the feast went on until
every last fish was eaten. There was no dessert after the Seven Fishes
Feast, just fresh fruits (oranges, grapes, melons and figs) and cheeses.

My brother and I fell asleep in the car on the ride across the
river to home and, barely awake, stumbled up the stairs to our
beds on the third floor, full of good food, excited about Christmas
morning at home and afternoon at Grandpa and Grandma's. I stayed
awake just long enough to say a prayer to Uncle Danny, telling him
that I would miss him tomorrow, miss hearing the Christmas songs
he always played on the piano as we opened our presents. I fell asleep
before I could finish my thought, how Uncle Danny played whenever we celebrated something,—or sometimes just as we were eating
our Sunday dinners. It seemed to me that he was part of everything,
even when he was somewhere else in the house. Would he still be
part of our Christmas? I knew we would think of him as we opened
our presents tomorrow, but would we think of him next year? And
would we stop thinking of him at all after some years passed? How
long would it be before we totally forgot about him, as if he had
never lived? Is that how it is when someone dies? Maybe that's why
Great Aunt Angie still wears all black after forty-five years since her
husband died—so she won't forget him, and so everyone will remember him when they see her in black in his memory.

There's so much to figure out about death.

Christmas morning at home was quieter than usual. My father
stayed in bed because he was especially tired and had a backache. We
had to be quiet because their bedroom was next to the living room
where the Christmas tree and the presents were. My brother shouted
when he opened the portable radio he had wanted, and I was very
excited about the Angora sweater I had admired when I saw it in
the window of the Rose Brandfield Ladies Store. I never dreamed
my mother even noticed when I said how beautiful it was on the

Saturday before Christmas when we were out shopping. Sometimes I think she is so amazing. She loved the pin we gave her— it had two hearts on it, one each from my brother and me. She said she would always wear it. She made us pizza fritta for breakfast, in the shape of stars, sprinkled with powdered sugar. And we were allowed to have cappuccino, which my mother made with a little coffee and mostly hot milk and chocolate, topped with whipped cream. My father got up and joined us for breakfast, but he was quiet, and just smiled a little when we gave him the presents my brother and I had gotten him. After breakfast, my father went to soak in hot water to ease his back pain. As my mother and I cleaned up the breakfast things, I asked about my father.

"Why is daddy always so quiet on Christmas? He looks so sad."

"Well, he is sad, in a way. You know, Daddy's mother died when he was still very young, and then his father married a woman who had a son. She was never very good to your father and his brothers, your Uncles Joe and Louie, and Johnny. Christmas was always a very sad time; no one got presents but their stepmother's son, and the rest of them had to work on the farm like it was just another day. He's very glad that you have a nice Christmas, but sometimes he can't stop thinking about the nice times he had when his mother was alive and the horrible times after, when his stepmother was so mean to him and his brothers—especially to his little brother, Johnny, who was so young and used to cry himself to sleep every night because he wanted his mother. It's hard to forget things that happen when you're a child, even many years later."

I was so shocked that my father had been so sad as a child and had been treated so badly. And my Uncle Johnny, who was always so smiley and jolly—I couldn't imagine him crying every night for his mother. When my father came back downstairs after his soak, I went to the living room, where he sat reading yesterday's paper.

"Thank you for all the beautiful presents, daddy," I said, sitting on the sofa near his chair.

"Well, your mother did all that. She knows what to get, you know."

"Yes, I know, but you always save money for the presents. She told me that."

"Well, that's what a father does, you know. But your mother knows how to pinch a penny. She saves her change all year long in a big old jar, just to have extra money for presents. She's a wonderful mother."

"Yes, she really is. And you're a wonderful father, too. We're very lucky to have both of you."

"Well, okay, then. Let me read my paper." He looked away, lifting his paper to cover his face, and said, "Doesn't your mother need some help in the kitchen?"

"Okay," I said, knowing he needed to end that kind of talk.

Later that morning, we set off for Newburgh and the Christmas party. The ferry was almost empty, and the morning so cold, that my brother and I didn't ask to stand outside.

As we rode the ferry to Newburgh, we told my mother and father about the Christmas Assembly we had at school on the last day before vacation, where the school chorus sang Christmas songs. My brother and two of his friends had sung, "We Three Kings." He had a beautiful voice and could sing the highest notes so easily. I sang with the sopranos in the chorus. We had practiced a beautiful Christmas song I had never heard before, "Away in a Manger," singing it in three parts for the assembly. I had sung the first soprano part. We were telling my mother about the assembly, when she asked us to sing for her.

So my brother and I sang our songs and other Christmas songs we had sung at the assembly, and my mother joined in on the songs she knew. Her voice was so clear and beautiful, and she knew how to sing the harmonies. She said she'd like us to sing for the family while we opened our presents at Grandpa's. We said we would, but she had to sing with us. She laughed, but never said she would.

One thing I really liked about Christmas at Grandpa's was that we opened presents before dinner. Even though there were a lot of us, it never took very long because everyone rushed through unwrapping each present, as the three youngest children played Santa, handing them out. My father always said it was like a madhouse.

Uncle Freddie arrived just as we were getting started. He was hauling his usual big box full of pocketbooks, and just as he was about to dump them on the floor in the middle of the parlor, there were loud voices from the kitchen, where my mother and my aunts were helping Grandma with the last-minute preparations for the Christmas Feast. Then complete silence.

The pocketbooks got dumped, and the three youngest cousins started gathering presents to distribute, when suddenly, a small boy with a head full of platinum curls came running into the crowded room, straight to the Christmas tree and the kids seated on the floor under it, yelling, "Merwy Cwissmiss! Merwy Cwissmiss!"

"Toomie! It's Toomie!" several of my cousins shouted, as he jumped on them, laughing. Standing in the doorway was Uncle Tom, smiling, as my uncles Nick, Mike, Freddie, John, Vinnie, and my father, all together, rushed to him, almost knocking him over, to shake his hand, embrace him, tell him how happy they were to see him. My mother and my aunts stood in the doorway, crying, watching Toomie with his cousins, who were giving him presents to open from a box filled with gifts that everyone had brought for him, with a plan that they would get delivered to Uncle Tom's house the next day.

My aunts came in, and kneeling around the pile of pocketbooks, began their selecting and swapping and arguing and bargaining as everyone settled in to the chaos of Christmas at Grandpa's, where the wrapping paper flew, and the Christmas songs were sung, and the wine was toasted, and the kids squealed with delight, and Uncle Tom laughed at his gift of a giant box of Corn Flakes, and Uncle Vinnie played Christmas songs on Uncle Danny's piano, and the long tables of glorious food, cooked so lovingly by the Aunts, celebrated these magical moments, when all seemed right in this Italian family, where great happiness and deep sorrow were held in equal reverence, with gratitude for the loving embrace of *"la Famiglia!"*

Coda

As I wrote these stories, I was once again living with my mother's family, reliving the events of their lives. Watching with my child's eyes even now, my memories are still those of the child I was then. How rich my childhood was, how funny and sweet and brave my aunts and uncles, how much I learned about life because of them.

How much I miss them and the world I was part of, the family I grew up in, the people so long gone—but so alive in my memory, in my heart. Telling their stories now is the only way I know to thank them for all the ways they enriched my life.

ROSEMARIE NAVARRA, born in Beacon, New York during radio days, began writing when she was nine—mystery stories featuring Peggy Blue, girl detective—solving every mystery on every last page.

A psychotherapist for forty years, she helped others unravel the mysteries of human emotions. During these years, she worked in community theatre with several groups as actor, director, and playwright.

She writes full-time now, mostly stories and plays, in a little college town, where people smile at the eccentricities of artists.

CPSIA information can be obtained
at www.ICGtesting.com
Printed in the USA
BVHW030121270221
601199BV00001B/121

9 780692 037263